Hacking the Human

This book is dedicated to
Ravinder, Alec, Oscar, and Mia

Hacking the Human

Social Engineering Techniques and Security Countermeasures

IAN MANN

Routledge
Taylor & Francis Group

LONDON AND NEW YORK

First published 2008 by Gower Publishing

Reissued 2018 by Routledge
2 Park Square, Milton Park, Abingdon, Oxon OX14 4RN
605 Third Avenue, New York, NY 10017

First issued in paperback 2021

Routledge is an imprint of the Taylor & Francis Group, an informa business

A Library of Congress record exists under LC control number: 2008019977

ISBN 13: 978-0-815-38938-5 (hbk)
ISBN 13: 978-1-351-15688-2 (ebk)
ISBN 13: 978-1-138-35704-4 (pbk)

DOI: 10.4324/9781351156882

Contents

List of Figures

Introduction

Information security is about people, yet in most cases protection is focused on technical countermeasures. This book is intended to help you redress the balance.

This is not a technical IT security book. There are plenty of those available in most good bookshops. This is a book for anyone wanting to understand more about information security, and specifically about the risks associated with targeting people – hacking humans. Social engineering techniques are specifically designed to bypass expensive IT security countermeasures, which they do often with surprising ease.

All the serious research into the methods used by attackers to compromise systems shows the human element is crucial to the majority of successful attacks. In many cases the attacker did not even need to find technical vulnerabilities, hacking the human was sufficient.

Who is responsible for your information security? In most organizations there are people with responsibility for IT security (firewalls, intrusion detection, anti-virus and so on) and other people with responsibility for physical security (doors, windows, CCTV and so on). So who's job is it to think about the people aspects of your security?

It may help to think about human security as the missing link between IT security and physical security.

There are a great variety of attacks involving social engineering: from tricking online banking users to enter their details into a fake site (this type of attack is known as 'phishing'), to gaining physical access to your organization through the manipulation of security guards and receptionists.

Most organizations focus almost completely on technical security. Attackers know this and often take the easy route to your confidential information – your

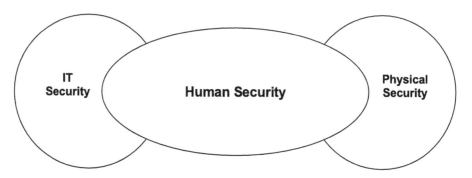

Figure I.1   Human security – the missing link

staff. With an expanding industry concentrated upon selling hardware and software 'solutions', this presents you with a real challenge in addressing your risks with appropriate social engineering protection, which requires an understanding of security process.

This book started from a series of seminars that I presented beginning in 2003. My extensive consulting experience included the investigation of security incidents, and building protection through the development of information security management systems. Time after time I could see that the human elements of information security were being neglected, and then exploited by attackers.

Seeing a problem isn't the same as finding a solution. This started me on a journey of discovery to establish why people can be manipulated with such ease. I asked, 'What are the techniques that are being used, and why do they work so well?' This investigation into the psychology of social engineering led me to a range of public presentations, and they have gained something of a following.

By addressing the problem of social engineering in a systematic way, and consequently designing equally systematic solutions, my colleagues and I have turned the 'black art' of social engineering into an information security risk that can be understood, measured and dealt with effectively.

In addition to developing this understanding for you, this book is designed to help you see that the solution is not merely a training issue. Although awareness building and training have a role to play, in many instances you will find that they are not the most effective solution. As you will learn from this book, susceptibility to social engineering attack is not correlated with lack of intelligence. We can all be targeted successfully.

Within this book, I set out to solve a number of potential problems that you may have with your social engineering protection. These could include:

- experiencing a number of incidents with a social engineering element, and seeing this as a significant weakness in your security;

- understanding the need to complement your technical IT security countermeasures with protection aimed at the human element of security;

- trying to assess the level of risk connected with the social engineering threat in your particular context;

- a lack of useful information regarding the human vulnerabilities that social engineering attacks tend to exploit;

- needing to measure the strength of your current security to withstand social engineering testing;

- wanting to understand the benefits, and limitations, of social engineering testing, and where it could fit into your information security management.

These are representative of the range of client problems that, in working as an information security consultant, I see on a daily basis. It is through this work that the observations, ideas, concepts and theories within this book have been developed.

The book is divided into three sections, with each of these comprising four chapters:

Section 1 – The Risks

CHAPTER 1 – WHAT IS SOCIAL ENGINEERING?

This chapter introduces you to some basic concepts of social engineering. By comparing the security approach of other information systems I show you how similar processes can, and should, be applied to the human elements of your information security. I explore a range of social engineering threats across a typical organization, and use the first incident example to show you just how easy it is to breach security using simple social engineering techniques.

CHAPTER 2 – UNDERSTANDING YOUR RISKS

Based on established risk assessment methodologies, I examine how you can identify social engineering-related risks to your organization. By taking a look at the way that people often misjudge risk, you can start to uncover the often illogical approach that the human brain takes to assessing risk. This helps to illustrate some of the challenges in conducting meaningful, yet realistic assessments of information security risk; particularly appropriate when trying to assess the human aspects of information security.

CHAPTER 3 – PEOPLE, YOUR WEAKEST LINK

Chapter 3 opens with an outline of some fundamental human vulnerabilities that are often targeted by social engineers. I have used a case study of breaking through a bank's physical entry controls to illustrate how some of these vulnerabilities can be exploited. Although largely ignored by the IT focused security industry, there is actually a long history of hackers exploiting people. They will target the weakest link in any security chain.

CHAPTER 4 – LIMITATIONS TO CURRENT SECURITY THINKING

Why are vendors of security products and solutions largely ignoring the human risks to information security? We also look at the organizational factors that hinder progress in developing effective security. By understanding the weaknesses in your current thinking and approach, you can begin to address the problem.

Section 2 – Understanding Human Vulnerabilities

CHAPTER 5 – TRUST ME

A fundamental process in many attacks is establishing trust. In this chapter we explore the latest thinking in this critical area, and look at the techniques that are effective. Through this chapter you can begin to develop your own social engineering skills. Understanding these techniques is essential if you are to effectively design the appropriate protection systems for your organization.

CHAPTER 6 – READING A PERSON

There are occasions when the skill of 'reading' another person can be useful in an attack. This chapter may also enable you to think of other applications of advanced mind-reading techniques; which leads on to the use of profiling techniques to begin to categorize people and predict their behaviour when subjected to certain attack techniques. Because like-minded individuals tend to make similar career choices, you can apply individual mapping across the organization. This can help you identify social engineering risks associated with different personalities. The chapter closes with a look at the techniques that can be used for some rather effective 'cold reading', useful if you fancy an alternative career as a psychic, astrologer or similar.

CHAPTER 7 – SUBCONSCIOUS MIND

Beginning with the application of some classic Neuro-Linguistic Programming (NLP) mind-reading techniques, this chapter takes you deeper into the inner workings of the subconscious. This may challenge your own beliefs, as we develop a model of the human mind, and establish some principles of decision making. This leads into the use of hypnotic language, and how our previously established personality profiles react and adapt to these techniques.

CHAPTER 8 – PARENT, ADULT, CHILD

The established field of Transactional Analysis can help you understand some of the dynamics of human interaction and communication. These can play a crucial part in the understanding of a range of social engineering attacks. The chapter relates some of the fundamentals of the Transactional Analysis discipline into information security attack scenarios.

Section 3 – Countermeasures

CHAPTER 9 – VULNERABILITY MAPPING

By understanding and developing the mapping of social engineering vulnerabilities within a given system, you can begin to identify where protection should be applied. This can help you understand where your strengths and weaknesses are, and how you can prioritize work to build effective protection.

CHAPTER 10 – PROTECTION SYSTEMS

What are the systems that can be used to build layers of protection to shield your vulnerable people? You can begin to understand where your current protection systems are already being effective, and where you need to build increased protection.

CHAPTER 11 – AWARENESS AND TRAINING

We deliberately give second place to training, in favour of the process of strengthening the systems that protect your people. Training does have a role to play. Traditional techniques can be flawed, in that they only target the conscious brain; providing limited protection when the attack is directed at the subconscious. This is an issue that will have been fully explored in Chapter 7.

CHAPTER 12 – TESTING

If you already test other areas of your information security, then the next step for you is to extend this to include social engineering testing. There are a variety of testing techniques that we have deployed in a variety of scenarios to highlight weaknesses in information security, and show the need for greater protection from attack.

Please do more than just read the book. You need to apply the concepts, and methodologies contained within these pages to gain the maximum benefit from the content. Your security problems are unique. The most interesting part of my job is understanding your challenges and designing the best solutions to help you. These pages will point you in the right direction, however the answer is not always simple. Sometimes complex problems have complex solutions.

Going Beyond Information Security

There are times throughout this book where you may notice me wandering away from information security and into the realms of human psychology. This is deliberate and you will see the benefits as we apply a diverse range of knowledge to the central challenge of securing the human. In understanding the ways that people are vulnerable to social engineering manipulation, you will find it helpful to observe many areas of human interaction for opportunities to test, or practise, social engineering techniques.

For example, as a consultant I have a very busy schedule, with plenty of travelling. This gives me many opportunities to concentrate on challenges such as writing this book. I find train journeys particularly good for this type of work. I often try to bring a little social engineering testing into long journeys. Currently I happen to be travelling home on a ticket that is half the price of a valid ticket for this journey, even though the ticket inspector has 'checked my ticket'. Before explaining the technique used to achieve this, I feel the need to give this some moral justification, so here goes:

- I bought the cheaper return ticket in good faith, not knowing that my return journey would be at peak (and therefore more expensive) time. For those readers not used to the UK train system, you need a degree-level education to understand the complexities of our current train ticketing system.

- I have not personally gained from this, as my client for today will be paying my expenses.

- I clearly offered my ticket for inspection, and was quite prepared to pay the cost of the upgrade if asked.

So assuming that you are satisfied with my ethics in this regard, let me explain the technique used.

A relatively well-known technique, particularly amongst magicians, is to distract you at a key moment in order to misdirect your attention. In this case the key moment is the specific point when the inspector views the (invalid) ticket. Using the knowledge that we shall be exploring in Section 2, I understand that the inspector will see what he expects to see, and if asked a question at precisely the right time, he is very likely to subconsciously carry on with the inspection, whilst consciously thinking about my question. In this case, the question was simply to ask what time we were due to reach our final destination. I also offered a subtle command to his subconscious, when finding the ticket in my shirt pocket, and offering it to him accompanied by the instruction 'this is the right ticket'.

If you are wondering how this works, then please reserve judgement until you have digested some of the deeper psychology within the later sections of this book. However, just to prepare you for the impact to come, it is worth pointing out that the same technique could be used with a completely blank piece of card instead of the ticket, with similar chances of success.

As you will see, examples from beyond the realm of information security can give us insight into how people can be manipulated to aid an attack.

A Note About Style

Rather than adopt a dry, formal and academic approach to this book, I have kept the style informal and relatively easy to read. There are a number of reasons for this:

- I want you to find the contents accessible. I may challenge much of your understanding, and even some of your beliefs, regarding the way the human mind works, yet there is no reason why complex ideas cannot be expressed simply, and this is what I have tried to do.

- Much of my work involves translating complex ideas and concepts into easy to understand information that can be used to get rapid results. I wanted this book to be the same. In many respects, this has been written in a similar way to how I construct a presentation or training workshop.

- In many places the text uses some of the techniques it describes, to be more engaging. You could even class some of the techniques used to be persuading. For example, a few pages ago the instruction 'you will learn from this book' was used within a sentence. This technique is deliberate and will become clearer as you proceed and learn some of the techniques for yourself.

- Finally, I wanted the book to be used beyond the obvious information security professional community. Many of the concepts are taken from, and can be applied to, other fields. This can include sales, marketing, information warfare, propaganda and even personal development.

Feel free to proceed with an open and inquisitive mind. I welcome your comments, experiences and challenges that you encounter as you develop your understanding of social engineering. You can get in touch to share these with me using my email: ian.mann@ecsc.co.uk

SECTION 1
The Risks

What is Social Engineering?

CHAPTER

1

A quick consultation with Wikipedia gives a definition of social engineering as, 'The practice of obtaining confidential information by manipulation of legitimate users.' This certainly captures some of the elements. At times it can be used to directly obtain confidential information, although all too often information hasn't been classified in any way, the target of the attack may not have even recognized the confidential nature of the information they are disclosing. However, there are other occasions when the action an attacker seeks may not be directly designed to manipulate you into disclosing information. Tricking a security guard into giving access to a building, using social engineering techniques, doesn't directly obtain confidential information – the objective may be to disable a facility and deny access to information.

The manipulation of legitimate users can play an important role in a social engineering attack. However, often you can trick an employee into going beyond their legitimate user rights as a route to your attack objective.

So a more appropriate definition, may be:

> *'To manipulate people, by deception, into giving out information, or performing an action.'*

This captures the distinctive aspects of targeting of people, and their manipulation, combined with the two main outcomes – direct loss of information and the achievement of some action desired by the attacker.

To identify specific improvements to your security it is vital that you can assess your vulnerabilities in a methodical way. Without this systematic approach you risk wasting investment in areas that are relatively unimportant to your overall security. If you understand the threats that your organization faces and have identified your specific human vulnerabilities, then you can target immediate improvements that offer maximum cost benefit.

Security professionals in the area of IT security have developed tried and tested methodologies for:

- identifying risks;

- detecting vulnerabilities;

- obtaining new information regarding vulnerabilities;

- developing targeted countermeasures based on risk assessments.

To give an established example; if you are responsible for the security of an Internet-facing web server, you can apply the above methodology by:

- Identifying areas of risk through the analysis of:

  - network architecture to understand the external exposure;
  - chosen technology platform, focusing on vulnerability history;
  - specific web applications deployed, and how they are coded;
  - administration and change control systems.

- Detecting vulnerabilities, either through penetration testing, configuration auditing or code auditing.

- Obtaining specific information regarding existing or new vulnerabilities related to each system component through established information sharing mechanisms and system vendor releases.

- Developing countermeasures by risk assessing new vulnerability information and available resources, such as vendor patches. This translates into:

  - a hardened web server that can withstand attack; and,
  - a protected web server, shielded from attacks.

Not 100 per cent secure, however secure enough – this is the basic principle of risk management.

The above accounts for the day-to-day work of thousands of security administrators around the world, supported by numerous available tools and consulting services.

Working with our clients, we show that a similar methodology can, and should, be applied to social engineering risk.

If you are serious about improving your security, then you must develop similar systems to understand and protect against human vulnerabilities as those currently deployed to protect your IT systems. The same methodology described for securing a web server can be applied to:

- Identifying risks in your information security, related to human vulnerabilities, through analysis of your systems; covered in the early chapters of this book.

- Detecting human vulnerabilities, through systematic testing. The established methodologies we use at ECSC are discussed in the later chapters.

- Sharing information to understand the human weaknesses that attackers can, and do, exploit. The main purpose of this book, and the subject of the majority of its content.

- Developing your countermeasures to give you:

  - resilient people, who are more likely to detect and counter an attack; and,
  - effective systemic improvements to reduce your reliance on people and their weaknesses.

As with our web server example, this will not make you 100 per cent secure. However, it is likely to be a great improvement on your current position.

With many attackers directing their efforts at obviously vulnerable systems, making your systems more secure than the majority under attack can be good enough. There are times when you may be targeted for other reasons, and your defences will need to be much stronger in these cases.

Unfortunately, humans are not as easy to secure as a web server. Fundamentally, however complex, with the right expertise an IT system can be understood. Human behaviour is much more complex. We have all been 'programmed' in infinitely complex ways, and therefore will react differently to the attackers' input. However, there are many human traits that can be modelled to increase our understanding and help predict their behaviour when under social engineering attack.

Fraudsters, hackers and tricksters understand this. They use knowledge of human weaknesses to guide them in designing new and more complex attacks. Because the success of these attacks is not guaranteed, they have traditionally carried a high degree of risk for the attacker. You can imagine the life of an old-fashioned con artist and the risk of being caught. However, the advent of the Internet, and the range of modern communication technologies, can give the social engineer the ultimate protection – distance and anonymity.

Let's take, for example, the 'phishing' attack we mentioned earlier; a relatively simple way of exploiting the average online banking customer's lack of security awareness and the banks' fundamentally weak systems, to steal your online identity. The attacker sends a fake email with a compelling reason for you to respond and links you to a realistic looking website where you log in and divulge your security details in the process.

Not only is the attack conducted from a distance (invariably from a previously hacked computer in a different country to the true attacker), it targets thousands of users simultaneously. The sheer volume of the attack means it doesn't even have to be very effective to reap significant rewards.

If a criminal attempts a face-to-face social engineering attack, they need to be either very good, or have a workable 'get out of jail free card' – we will discuss this in more depth when we look at testing methodologies. With a volume attack, such as deployed with phishing, you don't need to be very good to get a handsome return. Imagine, for example, you send 1 000 000 emails and only 5 per cent use the online bank you are targeting, and only 0.1 per cent fall for the scam. If you find £1 000 in each account compromised then you have just made £50 000, and that is with only 1 in 1 000 falling for the con.

The ease of such attacks explains why many attacks are not very well written; the early examples had numerous, simple mistakes in spelling and grammar. However, they worked to some degree and were therefore good enough for the attacker. We are now seeing more sophisticated attacks, with more applied psychology to improve the hit-rate, and fool even the most astute user.

Attackers now adopt more sophisticated techniques to target individuals in all organizations. Therefore we need to develop better understanding of human weaknesses and delve into the psychology of persuasion, if we are to counter them.

Social Engineering Threats

Many organizations, wanting to develop an effective Information Security Management System (ISMS), have looked to the ISO 27001 standard (previously also known as BS 7799, and ISO 17799). This is a broad international standard covering many areas of security, including IT, human resources, physical security and business continuity.

One weakness of the current ISO 27001 standard is that, although in many ways it is broad in its coverage of security, its recognition of social engineering is poor. With only minimal coverage on user awareness and training, it fails to direct people to a fuller understanding of social engineering threats.

Although, contrary to many peoples' beliefs, the standard is written on the understanding that you may well develop additional countermeasures, over and above the 133 controls currently in Annex A. Close examination of the current mandatory clause 4.2.1 g) reveals, 'Controls listed in Annex A are not exhaustive and additional control objectives and controls may also be selected.'

Therefore it is useful to map some social engineering threats to different areas of the standard to identify a complete picture of the risks.

HIDDEN INFORMATION ASSETS

At the very early stages of your information security risk identification, it is worth spending some time thinking about your information assets. This is especially valuable in thinking beyond the obvious paper files and electronic data. Particular focus should be given to knowledge that key people hold within their heads, as it is often the case that this information is crucial. You may identify critical IT systems that are largely undocumented and rely on the knowledge of key people who manage them, or in some cases wrote the software in the first place.

The type of information that is only held by key individuals can be difficult to secure as your control is limited. A social engineer is only one trick away from getting disclosure of this information, as physical and electronic access controls cannot be applied.

We are quite used to a narrow interpretation of assets simply being hardware and software. However, we do expect a realistic linkage to information storage, and/or processing. We recently came across some rather bizarre interpretation of what information assets are, in the context of an ISO 27001 implementation.

In one organization, a consultant had insisted that the projector in the client's boardroom should be included in the risk assessment. The client had rightly questioned this as they couldn't understand the significance for their security. Risk assessments should be formulated in a way that senior managers can understand the issues and make informed judgements.

In this case, the projector wasn't part of an important information system (they had a spare) and it didn't store information. The only, obscure, risk scenario they may consider is that they tended to present in the room with the blinds open to the car park, thus there was a conceivable risk that someone may view the contents. However, this was still not a good reason to start analysing the projector within the risk assessment. Better to keep things sensible and get realistic results. A useful test of the value of your assessments is whether they lead to new understanding, measurement or management action.

THIRD-PARTY RISKS

Many organizations underestimate the risk associated with third parties who can access their information. This is especially relevant where you outsource aspects of your operations, with third-party employees working on your site.

In many instances it can be relatively easy for the social engineer to either target third parties for information or assume their identity to gain access.

Established work practices can be an open door to an attack. With the growing compliance burden upon organizations, you may well be experiencing more and more audits. Assuming the identity of an auditor is a great way to gain access to information. Many people are effectively conditioned to allow anyone claiming to be an auditor to access any information, and often to take copies at will.

HUMAN RESOURCES

The personnel department can be a significant source of social engineering risk, as they are often responsible for establishing identity checks. If someone is going to the lengths of trying to gain access to your information by coming to work for you, then this could be your only defence. Although elaborate checks may not be feasible, and would certainly be too costly, for every role within your organization, you will be able to identify certain key roles where information access is so critical that you can justify enhanced pre-employment checks. It is important not to think that seniority necessarily correlates with critical information access. In many organizations quite junior IT staff have more information access than most senior managers.

It is also crucial not to neglect the employment exit process, as the following incident illustrates:

Incident

An executive PA had come into a company with a great track record, having had an identical role with a very similar organization. She had approached the organization as her husband had taken a job in the area and she was relocating. The company took the opportunity to hire her, especially as she was very impressive at interview with her knowledge of this industry sector. In addition she was willing to take a small pay cut to secure the position.

As is usually the case, she was given immediate access to the information she 'needed' to do the job, and was quite quickly given the login and passwords details of the director for whom she worked. This was also normal for PAs in her position. She impressed everyone with her knowledge, and with how keen she was to learn as quickly as possible.

Unfortunately she left after only 3 weeks, quite simply disappearing. Suspicions where only raised when attempts to contact her showed the details she had supplied at the time of appointment were false. Human Resources had not yet undertaken all the normal checks as 'she hadn't yet returned all the forms'.

Some careful examination of a variety of logs, show evidence that she had been systematically sending information out through emails to a variety of email accounts, and her photocopy usage appeared to be out of all proportion to her job requirements by a factor of about 100.

Discreet enquiries to the competitor, for whom she claimed to have worked for previously, did not yield any results. This is not surprising, as the only actual evidence of her working for this, one of many, competitors was her original letter offering her services.

Vulnerability analysis

It is quite 'natural' to jump at the opportunity to bring in someone to your team who has plenty of relevant experience. However, if background checks are important enough to put resources into, then they are important enough to complete before giving someone access to critical business information.

In our experience, sharing executive access control mechanisms such as logins and passwords is as common as it is stupid.

Possible countermeasures

The obvious improvements should be centred around the recruitment process. In this case, the way the executives rushed to appoint this apparently talented individual didn't help the Human Resources department. Some of the usual processes were bypassed by the senior managers.

Better access control to information could have limited the impact of this attack.

Further investigation showed that there were numerous opportunities to establish some early warning signs. For example, large numbers of documents attached to emails could be identified, and should have been investigated. These could have been used to detect this breach before it was too late. By the time we were involved, this client had very little to gain other than to try and learn from their mistakes. Catching the individual 'in the act' would have given much more scope to investigate, and potentially identify if an organization was behind

PHYSICAL ACCESS CONTROL

As you will see from various examples within these pages, the skilled social engineer can make rapid progress through physical security barriers, especially where there is a significant human element to exploit.

The physical security section of the ISO 27001 standard, and associated guidance, concentrates almost exclusively on security hardware, such as locks, keypads, alarms and CCTV. In our experience, it is the critical point of interaction between these physical controls and their human components that gives the opportunity for social engineering exploitation.

Contrary to popular belief, when testing physical barrier entry controls, I prefer to see the presence of security guards. Rather than adding security, they usually give you the opportunity to gain entry, as there are nearly always circumstances when they will allow you access through the barrier even though you don't have the correct swipe or key fob access.

Without the guards to exploit you are left with less choices, such as jumping the barrier (I was never very good at the hurdles), or activating some 'emergency' access switch (likely to gain unwanted attention). Or you may have to go to the lengths of walking around the building to find the back entrance that wasn't important enough to justify investment in a barrier. Failing that, there is often a fire exit somewhere in use by the remnants of the smoking community, who have been instructed not to stand outside the front entrance.

HOME WORKERS

Home workers make interesting social engineering targets. The threat can be twofold:

1.   The criminal can target them directly; particularly useful since their associated electronic security countermeasures (such as firewalls) are usually weaker than the main office facilities. So a combination of technical and human attack techniques can work very well. An example may be to trick them into opening an email and running an attached program. The attacker may also exploit their detachment from the organization. Long-term home workers are less likely to know, in person, someone calling from the office who has an urgent request for information.

2.   Their detachment can also be exploited in reverse. Assuming the identity of home workers can be a useful ploy to trick head office into divulging information. This is very effective when targeting helpdesks. Helpdesk employees have been trained to be especially helpful to those people working from home, who don't have as easy access to help and guidance.

ACCESS CONTROL

As in the case of the executive PA given all too easy access to the accounts of her bosses, in most instances access control is poor. In many client organizations, we find significant weaknesses, both in terms of overall design, and in particular with the ongoing management.

Without effective internal segregation of access, an attacker only has to find the single weakest human link in your security chain, and they can access the crown jewels of your most valuable data.

For most organizations, the number one reason why nobody is carrying out a proper review and analysis of their IT access controls, and associated permissions, is that these systems are so unstructured and unmanaged, that effective control is impossible.

It is a challenge to set-up, enforce and control the ongoing clutter and mistakes, and to avoid the compromise of an access control system that grows and develops organically with the network. Ask yourself one simple question: 'What is the proportion of requests to give more access to information, compared with the requests to remove access?' In many cases the answer clearly illustrates the pressure to gradually relax access controls.

Some organizations jump headlong into expensive 'solutions' such as biometrics. These are, at the time of writing, not, despite the vendors' promises, sufficiently developed to be used for more than a marketing veneer. In most situations, better management of the existing access control mechanisms can give much greater security returns.

Measurement of Security Controls

The meaningful measurement of security controls presents significant challenges. This is especially the case if you want to go beyond the most basic technical measurement, such as recording how many packets your Internet firewall is blocking. That is something, that apart from in a few particular instances, I am really not interested in. After all, we know the Internet is a dangerous place, and that any connection to it will be probed many times a day. Simply counting what is getting blocked does not give you useful information. The measurement of social engineering-related information security metrics presents even more challenges.

As a starting point, you should be tracking which incidents have a social engineering element. Although, it is widely agreed that most social engineering attacks go undetected, you should, as a starting point, begin to track where they are possibly being used in your organization. As your mechanisms for measurement develop, your risk assessment will become more meaningful, and accurate.

It may also be useful to establish some measurements through your ongoing testing of security. Your remote penetration testing, on-site vulnerability assessments and application/code testing can give you an ongoing indicator of the effectiveness of your IT security. Effective testing of your risk from social engineering can underline the benefits of improvements to your information security.

WHERE CAN YOU BEGIN?

Why is social engineering risk ignored, or neglected, in the information security procedures of many organizations?

- The business of information security is dominated by IT security hardware and software vendors. Whilst vendor products have their place (some may even improve your security!), they do not address your greatest weakness – people.

- Most information security improvements concentrate on technical countermeasures because they are relatively easy. We don't mean to trivialize the technical challenges in security. With the appropriate technical skills, the supporting management systems and the right technology, all technical problems can be solved. Humans are much more complex, less understood and present a bigger challenge in addressing security vulnerabilities.

Once you recognize that social engineering is largely ignored, and therefore an easy method of attack, you begin to understand your own weaknesses. The starting point is a more formal risk assessment process to help you prioritize the protection that you need.

Understanding Your Risks

I am a firm believer in a solid, methodical, approach to information security risk assessment. Time and again I see holes in an organization's security and money wasted in areas that have not been properly thought out.

An effective risk assessment approach enables you to target resources, commensurate with levels of risk. Thus, it is in all our interests to understand information security risk and do our best to help manage them, if only to protect our pensions.

Defining Social Engineering Risk

You will find it useful to put information security development within a risk framework. This is particularly valuable when communicating issues to senior management. The ISO 27001 standard defines risk as the 'combination of the probability of an event and its consequence'. Interestingly, this fails to capture the negative outcomes that we are associating with an information security risk.

Perhaps a more appropriate definition of risk, such as 'the possibility that something unpleasant or unwelcome will happen' provides a better starting point in our exploration of social engineering risk.

Two components are essential to the understanding of risk:

1. Impact – there must be some impact on the system in question. You could replace the word impact with damage. Without impact there is no risk.

2. Probability – if the risk is guaranteed *never* to happen, then again we are not interested. There must be some chance of an event happening to create a real risk.

Thus, the combination of some impact (however small) and a real probability (however unlikely) gives us a risk (however small).

We make use of impact and probability to discern which risks are realistic for you and your organization. Be careful, many risks can be overlooked because they are undetected or fall into the 'why would anyone target us' or 'it could never happen here' categories. It is worth remembering that a good reason to target you would be your mistaken assumption that nobody would bother.

Let's take an example, of a manager making an information security error with potentially large consequences. The associated weaknesses in security countermeasures could open the door to a social engineering attack:

Incident: Use of Web Email

We were called into a major plc, precisely one week prior to their annual results being made public to the London Stock Exchange. This organization was experiencing some challenging times. Although their turnover was in excess of £1 billion, their profits were wafer thin which was leading to speculation about takeovers. With management under pressure to deliver, the results were hotly anticipated. Movements in share prices of £millions was likely upon the results being made public. Anyway, to the incident.

As part of the preparation for presentation of results, the CFO had sent the CEO an email with the draft results attached. This had gone to his firstname.surname@hotmail.com account. Unfortunately, the CFO had then realized that the CEO actually used Yahoo email. The obvious concern was that someone else had now received their draft results, a week in advance of official release.

As is often the case, the managers didn't really understand their problem or have a realistic expectancy of what could be done to limit the impact of the breach. Their original idea had been to bring someone in to hack the computer of the individual who had received the email, to stop them using it. We pointed out that we could not help with this strategy, for two good reasons:

1. it is illegal, and therefore not within our portfolio of consulting services;
2. they would be digging themselves into a massive hole by turning a simple mistake into something more serious.

Following some initial investigations into the identity of the individual concerned, our advice was to sweat it out for the week. The chances were that the individual receiving the email wouldn't recognize its significance, as the email covering the attachment, didn't give too much away in that regard.

After a particularly stressful week (on their part) the incident disappeared as the information was made public. No out of the ordinary share movements, other than speculative trading, or disclosure of information had resulted; a near miss.

Vulnerability analysis

The use of public web-mail systems for transmitting any confidential information is risky. When asked why these systems were being used, the executives expressed a concern that the internal email system may not be secure, thus they preferred their private emails for confidential information.

They were certainly classifying information and recognizing its value. However, their understanding of risk, through an understanding of relative vulnerabilities of different systems, was lacking. Internal email systems are often compromised, usually by the internal administrators who find it too tempting to look at the communication between their managers.

Possible countermeasures

So what measures could this company have taken to prevent this incident?

- Stop using external public email systems. This assumes that the internal alternative is appropriate. It is a worthwhile exercise to look at the administration and access control around email systems. This can give executives confidence to use them appropriately.

- Better classification of information and associated rules as to its handling. This is more of a general countermeasure and not particularly effective in this case. I am sure you will have experienced the fact that senior managers are not always good at following such rules, and the rules would probably have made no difference in this case.

> • Use appropriate encryption between the executives. Not necessarily easy for them to operate, however, working on the assumption that executives are bright people, with appropriate support this can be achieved.

Working with web-based public email systems has another significant vulnerability – it is open to phishing type attacks. Because the registration of new addresses is open to the public, it is relatively easy to register user names such as:

incidentdetectionteam@hotmail.com or

securityfraudteam@gmail.com

I know these are easily registered, as I have just done it.

These can then be used to send emails to unsuspecting users, warning them of fraud and directing them to fake sites that will trick them into divulging their passwords. Then their email can be accessed at will.

The designers of public email systems really should do better. I understand that the economics of systems such as this demand a high degree of automation, yet this is often at the expense of security. There are plenty of key words in my two examples above, such as 'incident', 'fraud' and 'security', that should be detected and are worthy of investigation by the system administrators.

This is an example of a targeted, social engineering attack. It is also important to remember that emails traversing the Internet are rather like postcards written in pencil – they can be seen in transit, and can be altered. In the case of the incident above, the executives should have been clear about the risks of public email systems and have had access to more secure alternatives for their confidential communication.

However, when working with senior managers you have a number of challenges:

• They are (usually) extremely busy, and therefore often not open to changing their established habits.

- They are not always receptive to receiving IT (as they see it) related training. They are visually uncomfortable in asking for help, particularly from junior members of the organization.

Fortunately for myself and my colleagues, they are often quite happy to listen to consultants, especially if they have personally decided to commission our services. And, following a major incident, executives are all ears.

Once a senior manager understands the risks, and how their behaviour can impact on the organization, they are only too keen to help with information security. However, understanding information security risks can be a great challenge, even for many full-time security professionals.

Remember, most people are inherently bad at judging probabilities. Next time you take a flight, just look out for someone who is clearly very scared at the prospect of getting on the plane (it may even be you!). Now, if they were to be thinking clearly about probability then they should be much more scared of taking a bath, as the clear statistical probability of death is much greater in taking a bath than flying in a plane. Slippery surfaces, that also happen to be quite hard on the head, combined with soapy water make a lethal environment. I wouldn't necessarily promote the idea that you try to confront someone on a plane with the inadequacy of their own risk calculations, or at least not until your have studied Chapter 5 on developing your rapport building skills. Perhaps you should also take a look at Chapter 7 and understand the relationship between the conscious and subconscious, as making a conscious assessment of personal risk can still leave the subconscious feeling scared – as in the example of a phobia.

If we were good at calculating probabilities then you would not find anyone buying a lottery ticket. Someone has calculated that in the United Kingdom you are more likely to be hit by an aeroplane falling from the sky at some point in your life (presumably towards the end) than to win the jackpot on the national lottery this week.

There are many reasons why we are not good at making judgements about risk. Dan Borge in his excellent publication *The Book of Risk*, draws upon the work of Tversky and Kahneman to categorize reasons why our judgement is often lacking. His categories relate well to social engineering and information security risk.

OVERCONFIDENCE

This is our natural tendency to underestimate the extreme ranges of possibility. We look at our normal expectations and judge that certain events are too rare to be realistic. When we have a lack of knowledge in a given area, this tendency of misjudgement is increased. Many senior executives are overconfident about their organization's information security and underestimate the possibility of severe breaches (until it happens). Often incidents that are security related are hidden as just part of the day-to-day difficulties resulting from IT systems. The fact that serious incidents are usually 'covered up' quickly, and almost never made public, tends to distort the view that executives have of their levels of risk.

OPTIMISM

We are particularly prone to overestimation of our own abilities in a given area, and have a tendency to then link this to our ability to control events, as in the example of the relative risks of flying against taking a bath. In one case you feel in control and have a mistaken belief in your own ability to avoid an accident. Despite all the evidence pointing to the contrary, many managers believe they are in control of their IT systems and think security events only happen to other organizations. This optimism is particularly evident in the common 'why would anyone target us' syndrome.

HINDSIGHT

People have a tendency to rewrite history. In particular, their recollection of events often includes elements of prediction that didn't happen. In many cases the responses to an attack are pure firefighting, and have very little correlation with any pre-prepared plans. In addition, many people do not revise their risk assessments in light of each incident. This lack of review hinders your ability to improve and identify weaknesses in your current countermeasures.

PATTERN SEEKING

We don't like random events as it leads to us feeling out of control and subject to unforeseen consequences. Human nature has a tendency to add meaning where none exists. Therefore, we naturally try to add patterns to events. The negative consequence of this is that we often discount the random nature of real events as we cannot see any reason for their occurrence.

OVERCOMPENSATION

When we develop confidence in our risk management systems, it can lead us to take unnecessarily high risks as we overcompensate. For example, the presence of air bags (and other well-marketed safety features) in cars can lead to more accidents, as it tends to lead to a false sense of security and people driving too fast. This is combined with their optimism in their own driving ability. When was the last time you heard someone declare their driving as below average? (According to my understanding of averages, this should apply to half the people you ask.) This overcompensation extends to the whole range of information security risk countermeasures. I am often involved with the development of methods to measure the effectiveness of information security controls, as risk assessments often assume a countermeasure is 100 per cent effective. This is rarely the case. In the area of social engineering the most common mistake relating to this area is the belief that simple training and awareness campaigns will significantly reduce the risk of successful attack.

MYOPIA

Using realistic timeframes for assessing risk is important. Myopia involves the mistake of taking the recent past, and a view of the near future, as the only indicative periods for assessment of risk. The rate of change in information systems makes this a particular challenge. In the case of risk assessments for new information system projects, the final 'solution' is often far removed from the original design, and therefore the risks are often also very different.

INERTIA

To do nothing is the choice made on too many occasions, despite all the evidence pointing to this being the highest risk strategy available. The potential danger of making decisions often has to be overcome before movement is possible. When people ask me how long the information security client engagement process takes, I often say, 'Either 6 months, or 10 minutes'. In the case of the former, it is often the time it can take to establish a relationship and take a client to the point of purchasing service. The latter refers to the decision-making timeframe when someone is already facing an incident – just long enough to see if we can help or not, and how long it will take us to be on-site.

COMPLACENCY

Risks we are familiar with often appear to be reduced. The fear factor of events is often heightened by the unknown nature of the potential danger. You only have to look at the public reaction to a new disease or illness. Compare this with the attention that thousands of road deaths, or more common diseases, attract. The familiar risk is of little concern compared with the unknown. It is worth thinking about whether you are giving undue attention to new threats, rather than the ones with the highest probability of occurring and resulting in the most damage.

ZEALOTRY

Zealotry is the tendency to stick to one view of the future (and its associated risk) even when the evidence is strongly pointing to a changing environment, and ignoring the fact that developing a new strategy would be wise. Given that risk assessments can take some time to complete, you can see why people may have a tendency to stick with them, despite mounting evidence that they should revisit their assumptions.

So, as you can now see, taking our natural tendency to misjudge risk with a general ignorance of information security risks, and particularly in the field of social engineering, we have much to learn.

We are going to explore some methods to assess risk, however, for now I would like you to assume that you are in that enviable position of having compiled an accurate assessment of your risks. Once you are in that position you will be able to make decisions about what actions you may wish to take. In many cases these decisions will be based on the cost of the countermeasure, compared with the potential reduction in the likely cost of the risk. Your management choices can include:

- Reducing your risks by applying new or improved security countermeasures. Care must be taken to reassess the new risk as it is rarely removed altogether.

- Accepting the risk, following a balance of the cost of new countermeasures against the potential losses in an incident.

- Transferring the risk to someone else, usually by outsourcing or insuring. Be careful, as elements of the risk often remain, such as damage to your reputation.

- Avoiding the risk altogether by changing the way that you operate your information systems.

This range of choices leads you to your social engineering development plan and helps you to manage the remaining risks in your systems. These are your residual risks. Remember, your goal here is to manage your risks rather than imagine that you can remove them altogether.

If, like me, you have never been a fan of existing information security risk assessment tools, you may have already created something that works well for you. Complex software tools tend to be characterized by time consuming activities that generate plenty of paperwork, yet don't necessarily increase your understanding of risk, or give clear, timely and prioritized actions for improvement.

Our approach is usually to examine any existing risk assessment systems. We then build on these, especially if they already provide an established reporting mechanism for senior management.

CHALLENGES

By completing an assessment and then taking logical, objective decisions, you will be in a position to manage your risks. However, information security is rarely that straightforward. There are some significant challenges in measuring your risks:

- Some risks carry the potential for a global impact. Virtually no other modern threat can bring multinational operations to a halt simultaneously across continents. There are many scenarios that can have huge impact on your operations, however, they have quite low probability of occurring. Traditionally, the measurement of risks that have a combination of high impact, with a low likelihood of the incident happening, are the most difficult.

- Quality data is tough to obtain. Most people are at an early stage in developing their measurement of information security. Organizations often lack good quality historical data to help them make their assessments. In addition, few organizations share information regarding their security incidents.

- Keeping up-to-date with new risks is a challenge. It would be hard to identify any other risk environment that changes so rapidly. The latest data shows IT security vulnerabilities being discovered at the rate of more than 15 per day. Many of these do not have available fixes and the associated risks need to be managed. We are fortunate that social engineering risks are not developing at the same rate. However, as most current attacks are still not using particularly advanced techniques, you can expect the sophistication of attack to increase over time, as the levels of protection increase.

To help you overcome these challenges and produce coherent, understandable and usable information security risk assessments, we suggest a range of methodologies. In order to illustrate a range of approaches, I have chosen three starting points. Clearly, the actual implementation of these will vary from client to client. However, you will be able to see how they could be applied to different areas of your information security risk assessment process. Each methodology, developed through solving the challenges of our clients, has increasing refinement of process, and gives you a progression path as your requirements become more complex. The labels (foundation, standardized and quantitative) for these are ones we use within ECSC.

Foundation Approach

The Foundation Approach is a good starting point, particularly as the framework for a brainstorming exercise. However, it is not detailed enough for a main ISO 27001 (BS 7799) risk assessment. The approach allows you to express ideas and experience without getting too tied up in the terminology of the standard. It can establish a process that can lead subsequently to a more sophisticated approach at a later date.

As you can see in Figure 2.1, the process lacks the complexities of valuation, or too much specialized terminology. The goal here is to identify relevant risks, prioritize them, then take action. Improvements take precedence over measurement and analysis.

There are occasions, such as when managing an incident response, where the biggest risk is time. You can imagine that spending days on analysis in the midst of a security breach is not a great strategy. Quick, efficient understanding of areas of risk is the priority in these situations.

We also find this approach useful in helping to translate the results of auditing and testing into a meaningful management report. By identifying the

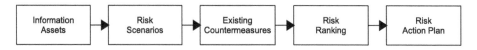

Figure 2.1   Foundation approach to risk assessment

relevant information asset, and linking this to a risk scenario, you can illustrate the impact upon the organization.

Existing countermeasures are important to take into consideration in prioritizing areas of risk. For example, if you highlight the ease by which a third party can gain physical access through a variety of routes, you should take into account any CCTV coverage that may act as a deterrent, potentially help detect intrusions or assist with any subsequent incident investigation.

Using the Foundation Approach, we are only interested in placing risks in the appropriate rank order, not in creating a relative measurement. It is sufficient for management to understand the areas of greatest risk. This is especially relevant to areas such as social engineering risk, where existing countermeasures are poor. There is little risk of wasting effort in security controls over and above those that make good economic sense.

As your information security management system evolves and you begin to build effective social engineering countermeasures in a number of areas, your risk assessment requirements will expand. You may wish to move to a system that gives you better management information.

Standardized Approach

To understand the Standardized Approach, two further terms are useful, particularly as you focus your attention on what constitutes a social engineering risk:

1. Threat – who or what is going to attack you? What is the potential cause of a security incident?

2. Vulnerability – what weaknesses do you have that could allow the threat to succeed?

Without both threat and vulnerability, there is no current risk. No threat can work on a system that is 100 per cent secure with no vulnerabilities (no system has yet been found that matches these criteria). Equally, numerous vulnerabilities could be present, however, without a threat there would never be a security breach.

To help people understand the relationship between threats and vulnerabilities, I often use the example of getting shot on your way to work.

Here I am talking about the risks of getting shot for the average business person in a 'normal' environment. If you are unfortunate enough to be working in a hazardous area where the example doesn't quite fit for you then please bear with me. The analysis is simple:

Threat: Getting shot on the way to work – very low.

Vulnerability: High, having not tried a 'penetration test',
                               I assume that I am vulnerable to bullets.

Possible countermeasure: Bulletproof vest.

Action: None, the threat is just too low. The cost of the
                               vest (and potential discomfort) outweigh the
                               perceived risk.

However, if I was travelling in a high-risk area, such as a war zone, I may well make a different assessment as the threat has just become real. Now the presence of threat and vulnerability combined makes a risk. So the bulletproof vest looks like a sensible countermeasure.

Equally, if I were Superman travelling the same route in a war zone, I would make a different assessment:

Threat: High – the lycra suit makes me an obvious target.

Vulnerability: Very low – I've seen the films and know that bullets just bounce
                 off.

As in our first scenario, we don't have significant threat AND vulnerability, so the risk isn't present.

This really is crucial to your process, to ensure you target countermeasures in the places they are going to give you the greatest return.

You may use the following methodology to meet the minimum require- ment for certification to ISO 27001 (BS 7799). The process described in the Standardized Approach captures the essential requirements necessary for certification.

As shown in Figure 2.2, you need to think explicitly about the value of your information assets, in terms of confidentiality, integrity and availability. This helps to give you a breadth to information security risk rather than a simple focus on secrecy of information, which is a common mistake. Although in the case of social engineering risk you may focus on the confidentiality aspects of your information assets, this is not always appropriate. Someone may be intent on disrupting your operation through an attack on a critical system availability – denying you access to your information may be as damaging as taking a copy.

The social engineering component of an attack may involve manipulating someone to perform an action that can assist with an electronic attack. For example, you may have a very effective Denial of Service protection system. However, a social engineering hacker may trick an administrator into disabling your protection, allowing the attack to proceed.

Splitting risks into threats and vulnerabilities allows you to distinguish between the elements under your control, the vulnerabilities, and the factors outside your control, the threats. This can give management a better understanding of how you can begin to manage the risks.

Using this approach, you are able to assign the information assets to appropriate owners. This is useful in bringing a wider middle management involvement in information security management. If you can help information owners to identify their risks, then you get better 'buy in' to the development, and ongoing management, of relevant countermeasures.

The grading of impact and probability is significant as it provides you with a measure of risk. This allows you to develop some objective criteria to base your management decisions upon and compare assessments over time.

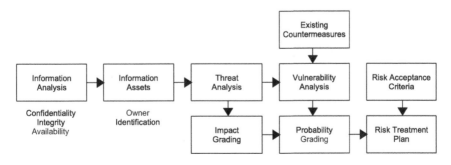

Figure 2.2   Standardized approach to risk assessment (ISO 27001 compliant)

Whilst offering compliance with the ISO 27001 (BS 7799) standard, and valuable management overview, this approach is still efficient and pragmatic. It gives you rapid results with a strong focus on proactive action.

Quantitative Approach

The final methodology moves you beyond the requirements of the ISO 27001 standard, towards the ideal of accurate financial measurement of risk, and objective decision making and reporting.

The goal at this level of assessment is to accurately measure each risk in financial terms. As shown in Figure 2.3, the precise loss associated with an incident (impact) is combined with its likelihood of happening (probability) to give a measure of annual loss expectancy. The benefits are immediate, as each investment in new security countermeasures can be judged objectively.

An additional benefit of this approach is that it can be effectively integrated with other established risk assessment systems and reporting mechanisms that use financial measurement as a key metric.

In principle, the quantitative approach sounds fantastic. However, there are challenges. The biggest mistake people make when presented with definitive outputs from such a system is to overlook that the inputs may not have been 100 per cent accurate. Remember, your input data gathering is probably still relatively immature. Management needs to understand the challenges that remain, and the complexities behind their clear, succinct, reports. The implementation of this methodology should be seen as an ongoing process, where the improvement of measurement is essential.

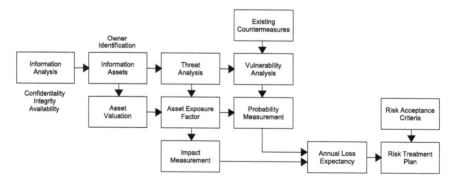

Figure 2.3   Quantitative approach to risk assessment (ISO 27001 compliant)

While so many attacks, particularly social engineering attacks, remain undetected, you need to be cautious in mistaking a relatively complex system for a perfectly accurate system.

People, Your Weakest Link

CHAPTER

3

Social Engineering Vulnerabilities

The purpose of this book is to go beyond simple illustrations of social engineering risk scenarios and help you to understand the underlying psychological weaknesses that lead to risks. What are some of the principal human vulnerabilities that relate to information security and are often exploited by a social engineer?

FOLLOWING INSTRUCTIONS

Whilst most people consciously believe they are independent thinkers, the reality is that it is easy to get people to follow instructions.

Last summer I was presenting at the annual British Computer Society (BCS) security conference in Birmingham. My particular presentation slot was after a large lunch, and the last in a group of three. The session before mine, which I thought very interesting, was a legal update. However, it was clear that the mainly technical IT audience had not come to listen to a lawyer and many were beginning to enter deep concentration (of the type that involves intently listening with your eyes closed).

I decided that I needed something a little different to get everyone's attention, so when I was introduced, rather than stay at the podium, I jumped down and approached the audience. Given that the audience consisted of about 150 people, I could be heard without the microphone. I started with, 'Now, I know many of you will have heard that I may be putting you into hypnosis in this session.' Actually, this was not the case at all. However, combined with me approaching the audience up close, it did get their attention.

I continued, 'I can assure you that I will not be using hypnosis,' not strictly true, depending upon your understanding of hypnotic states (more on this in later chapters) 'but to begin with could you all please stand up?' Now, with my obvious expectation of compliance, and my close proximity, everyone complied and stood. This uses, in addition to the prompting by me, an anticipated group dynamic. In addition, people in general want to avoid the embarrassment of being singled out, so once a few people start to stand up, the rest soon follow.

I then returned to the podium, and announced, 'In this presentation, we shall be examining just how easy it is to get people to follow your instructions. You can now all sit down.'

In fact, with the exception of the chairman, the whole panel had also stood up.

Despite our belief that we don't follow instructions, the reality is that for every time you refuse, there are literally thousands of times when you comply. From early childhood, through school, and into employment, we naturally follow instructions.

It is not by accident that military training involves intensive repetition in following instruction and acting as a group in compliance to senior officers. Drilling is exactly that, drilling the mind to be compliant to instruction. When given the instruction to attack the enemy, an army wouldn't function if individuals wanted to debate the merit of the particular strategy being suggested.

IGNORANCE

Most people are compliant to instruction when they feel ignorant about the situation they are in. Irrespective of your level of IT knowledge, you will recognize that the majority of people feel relatively ignorant of IT systems. This is especially the case when they feel that someone else knows more than themselves. Given that a high proportion of social engineers also have good technical knowledge, they can use this to their advantage in obtaining compliance. In most cases, a normal user will always follow an instruction when they perceive that it originates from an expert. Don't confuse this ignorance with lack of intelligence, it is a localized feeling related to the specific circumstances in which the target finds themselves in.

Nor should you fall into the trap of believing that social engineering only works against people of lesser intelligence – this is not the case. In my work with the UK government, I recently reviewed some official documentation where it was stated that social engineering was 'an attempt to exploit the naivety of users,' followed by the statement that 'education is the only effective way to directly protect against social engineering'. As you will see as we explore the issue in more depth, the author of this document is wrong in both cases.

This document went on to give the reassurance that a 'well-secured network' will reduce the impact of a successful social engineering attack. I see very little evidence to support this statement.

GULLIBILITY

An interesting characteristic of peoples' gullibility is that it tends to increase if they are offered increasingly attractive benefits.

One example is the 419 scam (the 419 refers to part of the Nigerian Criminal Code dealing with fraud) where you receive an email from a relative of an African prince (or similar) who has a plausible (NOT) story of millions of pounds that are tied up in a bank account somewhere. They have chosen you to help them simply transfer the funds via your bank account, for which you shall receive a 'modest' payment of perhaps a £ million. I am working here in pounds sterling where a million is still a tidy sum. Please feel free to add some extra zeros if your local currency is heading rapidly towards devaluation.

You may be thinking that this is now so well known that people cannot possibly be falling for it. However, in our filtering of emails, we still see a significant number of these, very obvious, attacks. Their consistent usage, with very little variation, is a good indication that people are still being caught out.

As you probably have heard, if you fall for the scam, as the promised transfer day arrives there is a 'small' hiccup that requires you to pay a small amount to receive the millions into your account. Of course the money doesn't arrive, and the hiccups get larger, as you are sucked deeper into the scam.

Some individuals have been lulled into paying out their life savings. There are a couple of interesting observations in relation to this particular scam:

- Even though this type of attack is so well known, many scams still say they are acting on behalf of someone in Nigeria. Enough people are still drawn in that the fraudsters haven't even felt the need to change the country in the story.

- In some cases where the police have got involved, the victims have blamed the police for stopping the transaction. Despite being presented with the truth of the scam, they still believe that the story was genuine and they were only days away from riches.

It really does appear that the greater the promise, the more our conscious logical processes give way to subconscious greed. Which is why more people can tell you what they would do with their lottery winnings than could explain the almost non-existent probability of them actually winning.

DESIRE TO BE LIKED

The desire to be liked is common to all of us and has been used by many sting operations. Foreign diplomats have, on occasion, been tricked into divulging information by the amorous advances of a particularly attractive individual. In a similar way to the breakdown of logic seen as financial gain increases in a lottery scam, a similar breakdown of conscious critical thought can often be observed in 'romantic' circumstances.

If you think back to our Executive PA incident, we did hear the same 'but she was so nice' from a number of the employees.

BEING HELPFUL

Being helpful involves more than simply holding the door open for people, which helps tailgating criminals to enter into your building. In a work context we are usually encouraged to be helpful to fellow employees.

Even office politics and conflict are usually put to one side in the case of new employees. As you think back to your first day in a new job, and how you felt, you will be extra helpful to that new employee who asks for help (for 'help', you can read 'confidential information').

Masquerading as a new employee is a particularly effective role for a social engineer. They are new and so you do not expect to recognize them. In addition, you would expect them to be asking for information, and do not particularly question any lack of knowledge of the way things are usually done; particularly good for targeting the IT helpdesk, where they have been trained to be especially helpful. In addition, the helpdesk staff are used to such routine tasks as resetting passwords – another useful avenue for a social engineer to exploit.

We will be taking these simple human vulnerabilities as a starting point and exposing them to a greater level of analysis throughout Section 2 of this book, as we explore the human mind and behaviour.

Let me walk you through an example of just how easy, by focusing upon peoples' vulnerabilities, it is to walk into the London head office of a major international bank, bypass all their security measures, and find yourself sat at a computer logged into the network.

The Risks Associated with Vulnerabilities

This following was achieved with just 1 hour of preparation and included bypassing a number of security countermeasures, including:

- police 'anti-terrorist' security check

- reception sign-in

- swipe-card entry system

- security guards

- internal entry controls

- IT network access controls.

CASE STUDY: POLICE 'ANTI-TERRORIST' SECURITY CHECK

I arrived in a black cab, dressed in an appropriately financial type suit, conservative tie, clean shaven, all designed to help with building initial trust. The large leather briefcase was ignored as it was obvious that I didn't look like a threat. To the heavy police presence in the City of London, I presented no obvious threat.

Reception

Our previous reconnaissance had uncovered a significant vulnerability: reception were giving out printed cards for visitors, permitting access to certain areas. These passes were then shown to the security guards to allow visitors through the swipe barriers. This potentially reduces the benefit of an expensive swipe entry system, simply to save employees from having to come to reception and escort visitors. I had arranged a prior meeting to see an employee which enabled me to retain the visitor badge and pass by avoiding handing them in when I left (I tailgated a group of departing employees).

Scanning the visitor badge and pass, with some simple editing on a standard PC, enabled duplication of the badge with the correct date for the intended social engineering test.

Risk 1: Will they change the colour of the pass each week/day?

This was a risk that I accepted. The threat was reduced with some diversionary tactics based on the security guard expecting the correct pass, re-enforced by approaching from the correct direction (reception desk).

The trick was to approach the security guard from reception. Having had a conversation that looked to the security guard as if I was signing in as an official visitor, I then turned, placing the badge on the suit as if the receptionist has just issued it. I kept the pass hidden as long as possible from the security guard in case it was the wrong colour.

Of course the conversation with the receptionist was a cover. I actually asked a question about whether she could tell me if another employee had arrived yet. A few other pleasantries made up the time of a typical sign in. She assumed I was an employee as there are so many she couldn't recognize them all. Also, I knew the turnover of support staff is high in this area of London. I kept my back to the security guard during this conversation. A quick observation of other employees arriving (the exercise was timed for 8:45am to give some cover) showed a number carrying takeaway coffees; behaviour which I copied, carrying a coffee into an office makes you look more like an employee than a visitor (or a threat!).

The security guard

I turned towards the security guard, pinning the badge on the pocket. This looked to the guard as if I were a visitor, and since my back was turned to the receptionist she still assumed I was an employee.

The pass to get through the gates was still a risk: had they changed colour, and had the guard noticed the fake? However, good use of the heavy bag and juggling a large coffee, allowed the pass to be shown only briefly. 'I've been told you have to let me up to the 12th floor' to the guard helped to reinforce what I required from him. You can rely on UK companies employing low-paid security guards, on long shifts, with little training. As an example of attention to detail, even my tie design was chosen to distract the guard away from the badge, and reduce the possibility of him spotting that the pass was the wrong colour.

The addition of a security guard was a security mistake. Designed to add security, he was actually the mechanism that enabled access.

Risk 2: Would the receptionist notice I had been allowed through by the security guard and not just swiped through as the employee she thought I was?

This was an acceptable risk as it was a busy time of the day and she probably would not notice. Most people in repetitive roles are working almost exclusively in the subconscious and don't notice things like this.

Internal entry controls

The difficult part was done. I was in the heart of the building with plenty of people moving around. I removed the badge in the lift, to become an employee again. Some simple tailgating with others allowed for free movement within the offices and through swipe-card entry doors.

I headed for the executive floor and presentation areas next. Here, some computers were helpfully left switched on and logged in with open access to the computer network.

Exercise achieved.

So, was this an exceptional example?

No! This is the norm in organizations, of all sizes, across all sectors. The required techniques may be different every time, yet the principle that security countermeasures are weak, and usually ignore the human (social engineering) element is almost universal.

Fraudsters have long recognized that people are the weakest link in security, and continue to target them, often in the home. One such scam involved the targeting of families in the US of serving military personnel. A telephone call informs them that they are due a $4 000 refund on their taxes. They are told they must pay a fee to cover postage, they are then asked for credit card details to cover the payment. A feature of this type of attack is that the individual amounts stolen are often small, yet apply to large numbers of people. This has the effect of often falling under the 'worth investigating' level of the criminal justice system.

In these, and similar cases, the attacker is assuming an identity that either generates trust or authority. We shall be exploring just how easy it is to convince someone of a false identity, and how quickly we trust what someone tells us as being the truth.

Let me further illustrate the weak links provided by people with a short story. This example reinforces just how hackers will exploit human weaknesses.

You should be able to spot similarities with your own organization, and where similar weaknesses may be found. I have called the target organization CriticalX. Clearly any resemblance to similar organizations is purely coincidence.

Attacking CriticalX

BACKGROUND

CriticalX are a young, entrepreneurial IT organization that have grown out of a web design company. Like many web design companies, they have responded to their client's requests, and moved into new areas of functionality. Skills in interface design have enabled them to sell a wide range of systems with some important functionality for their clients. They now employ 200 people and are growing rapidly.

One particular area of growth is the provision of a Human Resource system 'PeopleEasy' for a range of organizations. Their business model is straightforward, with web-based applications accessed across the Internet by their clients. They have found these systems relatively easy to sell, using the case study examples of high-profile clients on their website to attract new business.

A key feature of the sales process involves selling directly to the HR department. They are able to demonstrate the application quickly during the sales visit from any Internet enabled PC. HR departments are usually well aware of the need to keep their information confidential. CriticalX have recognized this, and make a point of highlighting the padlock in the corner of the browser when demonstrating the system to potential customers, as this shows the site is 'as secure as online banking'. This reassurance, however hollow, combined with an impressive client list, case studies and a well-designed application make a compelling case for a HR department. These selling points are delivered by a sales team that is conversant with the finer persuasion skills covered later in this book.

Another point worth noting here is that CriticalX are managing to sell into organizations with well-developed security functions within their IT departments. And yet, they never get asked security questions as part of the sales process. Why is this?

Very simply, the clients' IT departments never get involved in the commissioning or implementation of this system. Implementation doesn't require the IT department (used as a key selling point by CriticalX) which means that any nominal security controls around system acquisition can be conveniently bypassed.

WHY TARGET CRITICALX?

Why would this small organization be of particular interest to a skilled attacker, HackerZ? Because of their clients; holding all the relevant human resource information about an organization can make you a key target.

In this case the ultimate target is not CriticalX at all, but one of their clients. The attacker is constructing a large, and relatively complex, attack on BankY (a large and attractive target). The attacker, recognizing that the human element of an attack will be crucial, is building up a profile of BankY's employees. A first step in constructing a social engineering attack is to identify key suppliers. CriticalX's online case studies, including details of the service supplied to BankY, is of particular interest. A little research on CriticalX shows them to be a small company, with rapid growth, and HackerZ has reasons to suspect that they may be an easier route into BankY, rather than a direct attack.

Note: although this assumption is common amongst hackers, there is very little correlation between organization size and the level of information security protection. Although size brings resources, and often expertise, it also brings complexity and significant inertia against change and response.

CRITICALX VULNERABILITIES

As with many organizations, CriticalX has neither identified, nor classified, its critical information – in this case, the client data. Access to critical systems is too widespread amongst their users, with poor controls over passwords. Real data is often used in test environments without controls over its usage and, more importantly, its deletion. This can open a system to a variety of technical hacking attacks towards multiple data points.

However, HackerZ has a different tactic in mind. She assumes, from the information on the website, that BankY is the largest, and most important, client of CriticalX. Therefore, it is reasonable to assume that serving the needs of BankY will be of prime importance. So why not social engineer CriticalX into simply sending the HR information directly to her? She has a plan:

- establish a relationship with CriticalX;

- gain their compliance with innocent requests for information;

- create an emergency to obtain the critical data.

CONTACT 1: WEDNESDAY 7:30PM

HackerZ: Hello, can I please speak to the helpdesk?

JohnnyT: This is the support desk, can I help you?

HackerZ: Oh thanks, this is Sarah Clark calling from BankY. I haven't called you before, but is this the right number for help with PeopleEasy?

JohnnyT: Yes, this is the right number Sarah, what is the difficulty?

HackerZ: Well, you will have to forgive me, as I am quite new in this role. I am doing some analysis and need help with summary reports. I work mainly from home, and tend to catch up with things once I have put my daughter to bed. I am so glad that you are still available to help me. Tell me, do you always work this late?

JohnnyT: Yes, I am the lucky person who covers the 7pm to 7am shift on Monday to Thursday.

HackerZ: So is it okay if I call you at this time? Sorry, I didn't get your name?

JohnnyT: Johnny. Yes, that is fine, your support contract is 24/7, and to be honest it can get a bit dull through the night. Call me at 3am if you want.

HackerZ: [Laughs]. Okay Johnny, I might just do that if Jessica gets me up like she often does. Mind you, I wouldn't normally be doing work at that time. I don't envy you working through the night.

JohnnyT: Well, it has its advantages. At least there are no bosses to interfere with things. Also, I tend to get longer to sort out your problems out of normal hours because it's not as busy. Anyway, what is your problem with summary reports?

HackerZ: Oh yes, sorry I forgot that I needed some help. Yes, summary reports. Well, as I said Johnny, I am quite new to this. I am just not sure how to run a report for a department to get our usual employee summary.

JohnnyT: Well, are you in the reports section?

HackerZ: Yes, I think so. I have searched for reports, but get lots of results. I'm not sure which is the best.

JohnnyT: Oh yes, much better to go to the management tab, then select reports.

HackerZ: Thanks. I can see you are an expert at this. Lucky I called you.

JohnnyT: Thanks, but at this time, its only me.

HackerZ: Okay I can see the reports listed. Are these reports we have set up?

JohnnyT: Yes, I have done some work for you guys, creating reports. Mainly for Jim Harrison.

HackerZ: Oh yes, I haven't met Jim yet, but I know he has done some work setting this up.

JohnnyT: Yes, you should find a tab for each department. Which one do you need?

HackerZ: Well first I was going to just query our service desk staff. But at the moment I am just experimenting to get used to the system. I am sure Johnny you know what it is like when you are new into a job. I want to keep one step ahead. It isn't easy, especially when you work from home like me. It can get a bit lonely at times.

JohnnyT: Tell me about it.

HackerZ: Okay, that has worked. Great. Might call you again later if that is okay?

JohnnyT: Sure, anytime.

HackerZ: Great to talk to you. Thanks.

ANALYSIS

So, what has HackerZ obtained so far? Very little, you may be thinking. Actually, she got exactly what she wanted from this first call – establishing a relationship. The information she gleaned was a bonus. However, in her experience, she expects to find new information from each contact with the target, it even adds to the excitement.

On the face of it, this was just another support call. However, let's re-run the call and explore what is really happening.

Before we start, it is worth noting that HackerZ: at no time had any access to the system PeopleEasy. A lesser-skilled attacker may have gone straight in trying to trick Johnny into giving her an account. However, that has risks, as there may be some strict procedures around this, and as yet, HackerZ: hasn't enough information with which to assess if this strategy may work.

So let's re-run the conversation to explore what really happened:

HackerZ: Hello, can I please speak to the helpdesk? **JohnnyT**: This is the support desk, can I help you?	*Comment: Although she got the title wrong, as a new employee this is understandable.*

HackerZ:	Oh thanks, this is Sarah Clark calling from BankY. I haven't called you before, but is this the right number for help with PeopleEasy?	*Comment: HackerZ has established that she is from BankY. This hasn't been challenged at all, so she now knows that authentication for support calls is weak. As she hasn't called before, she may have been*
JohnnyT:	Yes, this is the right number Sarah, what is the difficulty?	*instructed that there is a procedure to register in order to get support. Currently, with no such procedure, she can proceed. If there was a procedure, she could have simply asked for help, and got details of what she would have to do.*
HackerZ:	Well, you will have to forgive me, as I am quite new in this role. I am doing some analysis and need help with summary reports. I work mainly from home and tend to catch up with things once I have put my daughter to bed. I am so glad that you are still available to help me. Tell me, do you always work this late?	*Comment: HackerZ has gained some sympathy and in the process found out the shift pattern for out-of-hours support. Also, the days Johnny works. She has mentioned summary reports. She knows they exist, because screen shots and feature lists from the website have highlighted them as a key benefit of PeopleEasy. From her analysis of CriticalX she guessed they wouldn't have many staff out-of-hours. However, this feature is*
JohnnyT:	Yes, I am the lucky person who covers the 7pm to 7am shift on Monday to Thursday.	*probably required when offering a system to an organization such as BankY.*

HackerZ:	So is it okay if I call you at this time? Sorry, I didn't get your name?	*Comment: The main objective here for HackerZ: is to develop rapport with Johnny. Getting his name is important, as using someone's name in conversation is a powerful way to develop communication. In the process, he has revealed that there are no management on-site through the night.*
JohnnyT:	Johnny. Yes, that is fine, your support contract is 24/7, and to be honest it can get a bit dull through the night. Call me at 3am if you want.	
HackerZ:	Laughs. Okay Johnny, I might just do that if Jessica gets me up like she often does. Mind you, I wouldn't normally be doing work at that time. I don't envy you working through the night.	
JohnnyT:	Well, it has its advantages. At least there are no bosses to interfere with things. Also, I tend to get longer to sort out your problems out of normal hours because it's not as busy. Anyway, what is your problem with summary reports?	

HackerZ:	Oh yes, sorry I forgot that I need your help. Yes, summary reports. Well, as I said Johnny, I am quite new to this. I am just not sure how to run a report for a department to get our usual employee summary.	*Comment: In addition to re-asking for his help, she reminded him that she is new to this job, and gained more sympathy in the process.*
JohnnyT:	Well, are you in the reports section?	
HackerZ:	Yes, I think so. I have searched for reports, but get lots of results. I'm not sure which is the best.	
JohnnyT:	Oh yes, much better to go to the management tab, then select reports.	
HackerZ:	Thanks. I can see you are an expert at this. Lucky I called you.	*Comment: Praising Johnny is a good tactic. Everyone likes praise, and tends not to get enough of it. He has now told her the name*
JohnnyT:	Thanks, but at this time, its only me.	*of a key contact (this may be of some use in the future). Her reply merely repeats back the same*
HackerZ:	Okay I can see the reports listed. Are these reports we have set up?	*information, yet sounds like she is an employee. She doesn't go as far as claiming to know Jim well. This could be risky, and may lead*
JohnnyT:	Yes, I have done some work for you guys, creating reports. Mainly for Jim Harrison.	*to a silly mistake. It is a good communication strategy to confirm the same information back at this stage, and better to be cautious on*
HackerZ:	Oh yes, haven't met Jim yet, but I know he has done some work setting this up.	*the first call.*

JohnnyT:	Yes, you should find a tab for each department. Which one do you need?	*Comment: HackerZ doesn't push things too hard. Johnny is now convinced she is looking at the system. They have also 'made friends', and opened the door for further communication.*
HackerZ:	Well first I was going to just query our service desk staff. But at the moment I am just experimenting to get used to the system. I am sure Johnny, you know what it is like when you are new into a job. I want to keep one step ahead. It isn't easy, especially when you work from home like me. Can get a bit lonely at times.	
JohnnyT:	Tell me about it.	
HackerZ:	Okay, that has worked. Great. Might call you again later if that is okay?	
JohnnyT:	Sure, anytime.	
HackerZ:	Great to talk to you. Thanks.	

HackerZ makes two further calls, in each case developing the relationship further, whilst asking for simple help that she can reasonably expect from the information gleaned from the website. She is careful to call when Johnny is on duty.

Still not pushing for a new account to be created, HackerZ probes for something potentially critical during call three. We join the conversation towards the end, after Johnny has helped her out:

CONTACT 3: MONDAY 9:30PM

HackerZ: Thanks Johnny. You are great at helping me when I need it. I bet you have to deal with much more complex problems than my silly requests.

JohnnyT: Well, it does vary. But most people are not as nice as you. But yes, the other night I was running custom SQL queries directly from the database for Jim.

HackerZ: Wow, not sure what that is, but sounds complicated. Can you pretty much do anything then?

JohnnyT: Yes, the system's not that difficult when you've been at it for a while.

As HackerZ suspected, Johnny has full administrator access directly to the data. This kind of access is common for support staff, and not just in small organizations. Unfortunately it is evidence of lazy access control. Johnny should be able to do 99.9 per cent of his job without full access to the data. Just think whether you would be giving someone in Johnny's role access to your HR files if they were paper records within your office?

This gives HackerZ a clue as to the way she can get to the data. Her fourth contact is the critical one. Remember, by this time Johnny 'knows' Sarah (HackerZ).

CONTACT 4: TUESDAY 5:00AM

The timing is deliberate. Johnny is at the start of a week of shifts. Following the weekend, this may well be the hardest time, as his body adjusts to night work. Also, late in the shift, he is likely to be tired.

HackerZ: Crying ... Oh Johnny, sorry to call you. It's Sarah again. Don't know what to do. I'm in a real mess here.

JohnnyT: Its all right, can I help? Sarah, don't cry, I'll do my best.

HackerZ: I don't know what to do. I've got to get this information for first thing. I've been up half the night with Jessica, and now it won't work.

JohnnyT: What's wrong? Tell me the problem, and I'll see what I can do.

HackerZ: I don't think you can help me. It just won't work at all. I should have done this yesterday. My boss will probably fire me if I don't have it for the morning. He's already been having a go at me for that time off with Jessica last week. He thinks working from home is easy. I've no one to turn to when it goes wrong. If you can't save me Johnny, I don't know what I'll do.

JohnnyT: I'll do my best. Just tell me the problem Sarah, and we'll sort it out.

HackerZ: I can't get anything to work. My computer's playing up and Explorer won't come up. I've rebooted about 50 times. I know you are great at helping, but I've only really used spreadsheets before. At my last job they taught me to do loads of things with spreadsheets. Now I can't even get into PeopleEasy. What can I do?

JohnnyT: Oh, I don't know. You say you can't open Explorer. This is the only way into the system. Are you sure it won't work?

HackerZ: [Crying] ... I've told you it won't work. I have to get these figures. I need lots of reports. I've got to summarize all this information. If only it was here in a spreadsheet I could do it in time. [Crying] ...

JohnnyT: Sarah, don't cry. You say, if you had a spreadsheet you could do what you need to do?

HackerZ: Yes, I think so. It's just that I need all the information. Can you help me Johnny?

JohnnyT: Look, I can get you that information. The database is really quite simple. I can make you some spreadsheets with everything you need.

HackerZ: [Still sobbing] ... Really? Wow, you are wonderful. Can you do that? I know spreadsheets. You've just saved my life.

JohnnyT: Look, I can get everything you need into some spreadsheets and email them to you.

HackerZ: Oh. Can you send them to my personal email, as BankY's system has been down since yesterday. That's partly why I'm still here at this time trying to get things done. I need to set off to work in a couple of hours, and my mother is coming round to take Jessica first thing.

JohnnyT: Can you explain what you need?

HackerZ: Johnny, I'm not too sure. Just put it all in a spreadsheet and I'm sure I can sort it out. You are a life saver!

As you can imagine, a number of spreadsheets duly arrived, containing a wealth of information about BankY's employees. HackerZ has achieved her objective of obtaining the HR information. Her original intention was to be able to profile individuals within critical BankY roles to aid her larger attack on BankY systems. However, in this case she discovered a bonus. The HR records included bank account details of each employee. One feature of PeopleEasy is that clients of CriticalX can configure their own fields. In this case BankY had extended the functionality to include an essential element of their payroll processing.

This is a really nice bonus for HackerZ. She can either make use of these bank account details, along with the other personal information to help her conduct fraud against many individuals' bank accounts. However, she has the bigger target of BankY in mind, so she decides to keep the information, as she can always sell it within the underground market. Always useful if she needs some extra funds to help her larger, and more ambitious, target of BankY.

VULNERABILITY ANALYSIS

BankY has made some fundamental errors in the commissioning of a new information system. By allowing the HR department to independently purchase and configure a system, they have effectively bypassed the usual information security controls of the bank. The external storage of such confidential information should be carefully considered, with appropriate controls agreed with the supplier. In addition, independent testing and/or auditing of these controls would be a sensible step to ensure compliance, and measure the effectiveness of the controls.

Putting the PeopleEasy system through a security review process should also have included an analysis of the information to be stored within the system. This should have highlighted the high risk of payroll information being stored, with personal details, in an externally managed system.

CriticalX has some fundamental weaknesses in its support processes. The first weakness is the lack of suitable authentication of support requests.

Secondly, no rules were in place to prevent JohnnyT sending the information directly to 'Sarah'.

POSSIBLE COUNTERMEASURES

For CriticalX there are a number of improvements that could be made:

- Establish an authentication system for support requests. This could involve maintaining a list of approved people who can make a call. Authentication could be achieved with some form of password, or a callback to designated numbers.

- Client information within PeopleEasy should be classified, with appropriate access control applied. Does JohnnyT really need full access to the database? 99 per cent of his support calls are likely to be limited to simple training of users in the correct operation of the system.

- Where it is appropriate to exchange data with a client such as BankY, outside of the system, appropriate secure transmission should be agreed. This may be encrypted email, or a secure download section within PeopleEasy.

- Finally, service desk administrators are prime social engineering targets. Some awareness and training to Johnny could have allowed him to be alerted to the attack – 'emergency' calls should lead to questions being asked. In this case, the request to send everything in a spreadsheet to a non-BankY email address should have generated an alert.

The last point sounds obvious, however it does require JohnnyT questioning the identity, and honesty of 'Sarah', who is now quite a good friend. Even with extensive training, his 'belief' in her could easily override this.

One of the most famous hackers to date was Kevin Mitnick. He gained more notoriety for his imprisonment without trial in the US, and the frankly ridiculous things said about his danger to society, than his actual hacking exploits. You should always show a healthy scepticism about a hacker's own stories, especially those that get caught. By definition, if they have been caught then they aren't necessarily the best at their chosen career path. However, what is interesting about Kevin is his admission that the social engineering part of his hacking was so important. When later giving evidence to the US Congress he stated that he 'was so successful in that line of attack' that he 'rarely had to resort to a technical attack'.

I am always interested in how easily social engineering techniques can be learnt. Large gatherings of people allow you to experiment with techniques on a greater number of participants. Recently we tried such an experiment:

Incident: Unlimited Free Alcohol

Each year ECSC exhibits at Infosecurity Europe in London. This is a great opportunity to meet with clients, and get an update on new offerings in the information security industry.

For the last few years, I have done a series of seminars and workshops on social engineering. This has given me a great opportunity to share techniques and methodologies from this book as they are developed. However, I have also managed to gain a modest following, who expect something new, interesting and amusing each year.

Therefore, recently, we decided to give free drinks to everyone.

The Infosecurity Europe show is great fun, usually a Tuesday, Wednesday and Thursday. Unfortunately, the Thursday is a little subdued, as the organizers put on a free drinks party for the exhibitors on the Wednesday evening, with as much free alcohol as you can drink, starting at 5:30pm. I am sure you can guess what IT salespeople + free drinks + 5:30pm start time equates to.

Coincidentally, my social engineering presentation was scheduled for 4:45pm to 5:15pm on the same evening.

Given the circumstances, I thought it only fair that I should invite all the delegates (approximately 100 people) from my presentation to join us for the free drinks. A great opportunity to try a little mass social engineering (can you have a little mass?), to see if we could get a large number of delegates past the security guards, whose job it is to ensure that only exhibitors gain access to the party.

In convincing colleagues, I had to come up with some moral justification, and this is it. Given that the drinks are free, nobody is losing financially. Also, I would be making a positive contribution to the state of the exhibition the following morning, as less alcohol between the exhibitors would mean lighter hangovers. In addition, we would be moving human knowledge of social engineering forward another step. (Okay, that last point is probably a little exaggeration.)

So, to the exploit. The only discernible difference between the badges of exhibitors and delegates was a nice red strip across the badge holder. There were other differences, but conveniently the red stripe obscured these. Therefore, the plan was to doctor the badges and help people gain access.

Step one: we conveniently left a number of red marker pens under delegate chairs. These had been selected to be a reasonable match, however not so great as to remove the element of risk, and therefore fun.

Step two: a mind script. Given the limited time to prepare people (the last two minutes in my presentation), we couldn't go through an in-depth course in getting past security guards. So I invited the delegates to imagine what it must feel like to be standing in an exhibition hall for two full days, and then to be offered unlimited free drinks. So diligently showing their badges would not be normal, more like a mad rush, desperate to get to the bar first. Better not to show the badge at all, and if challenged, annoyingly flash the badge towards the guard. The red flash will be sufficient to satisfy the guards.

Did we succeed in this social engineering experiment? Certainly by the number of people who I met throughout the evening thanking me for their drink. I even managed to get a rather nice photo of three 'consultants' from one of the big four audit firms, holding up their fake badges, together with fists full of beer bottles. They were obviously intelligent enough to follow my instructions and gain entry. Unfortunately, they weren't quite intelligent (or sober) enough to refuse to have their photo taken with badges that clearly identified them by name and company. Anyway the photo makes a nice addition to my presentations on the subject. I am sure you can forgive me for slightly exploiting fellow consultants.

Vulnerability analysis

This was another example of security guards working in the subconscious, blindly accepting badges with only a cursory glance to check for a colour.

Given the subject of the exhibition, and its attendees, it would be nice to see rather better security measures in place.

Possible countermeasures

1. Remember, coloured badges are often a terrible idea, as they lead to people judging them purely on colour, and not examining the details.
2. Security guards doing more than just giving the feeling of security, or satisfying the minimum requirements of insurance policies.

Limitations to Current Security Thinking

CHAPTER

4

As my role involves working with managers at all levels, and many people working within information (and IT) security, I have had many chances to observe why social engineering is largely ignored by so many people.

Given the numerous examples of the use of social engineering going on, building on a tradition of confidence tricksters, it is difficult to argue that the phenomena is a new one. So what are the factors that are leading to this important area getting very little attention?

Information Security Vendors

Many vendors of hardware, software and services now talk about information security, rather than just IT security. Unfortunately, this may be more about linking their products to the latest issues, such as ISO 27001, in order to sell more, rather than about a genuine interest in security information.

Social engineering problems, often requiring complex human solutions, are just not attractive to most organizations looking to make money from information security products and services. Therefore we see a market place dominated with technical solutions promising much in the way of security, whilst, despite evidence to contrary, ignoring the human element.

Organizational Structure

Currently, in the majority of organizations, the responsibility for information security resides within the IT department. This is largely historical, and has usually resulted from the development of IT security into information security.

As we look at social engineering risk, which brings together IT, physical security and a large slice of Human Resources, it is clear that simply dumping it in the hands of the IT department is insufficient.

Many people end up in an IT role because they enjoy technology. If they wanted to work with people, they would be working in Human Resources. So if you are a manager, with responsibilities that include information security, think about the mix of people within your teams. Are they giving you the right balance between physical, IT and human security? You may need to think about recruiting a psychologist!

Security Professionals

Currently, the breadth of professional knowledge in information security is thin on the ground with any in-depth social engineering content. In researching for this book, I was surprised at how the same, quite simple, messages that 'you must train your users' is rarely expanded upon.

I do believe strongly that, as security professionals (and I hope many of you will be reading this text), we should ensure that the right balance is achieved between different areas of information security risk. This means that we need to address social engineering issues as part of our solutions. If we promote solutions that do not serve the organization's needs, we will simply be moving the industry backwards, and making life even easier for the attackers.

We cannot expect the average user of systems to understand the threats to their security. The attackers will always be ten steps ahead of the user. We have to ensure that the systems we design can withstand attack and protect the user. Until we do so, the users will be vulnerable, as can be seen in the following example:

Incident: Credit Card PIN Technique

You may look around your office, and see opportunities for someone to steal credit and debit cards. Perhaps jackets with wallets in the pockets, or the odd bag left near a desk. These items are relatively easy to remove in this context. However, to be really worth the risk of getting caught stealing these items the thief needs the PIN number, so a little more ingenuity is required.

Imagine you get a call at work: 'Hello XXXX, sorry to bother you at work, but this is an emergency. I am calling from BANKX regarding your credit card number XXXX XXXX XXXX XXXX. We have detected a number of transactions this morning from your account that we suspect are fraudulent. Do you have the card in your possession?'

You check, only to find that your wallet/purse is missing.

'Don't worry Sir/Madam, you are protected by our new Fraud Protection Service. I can cancel your card immediately, cover these losses and get a new card out to you within the next few days. I just need to take you through security and we can sort this out for you.'

The process of taking you through security involves the usual types of questions. However, in this case it also involved asking for the person's personal identification number (PIN). Perhaps not a usual request, however in the circumstances it was 'required' to instigate cancelling the card rapidly.

Sounds convincing, and most people would be taken in. However, the above example was used by thieves who had stolen the credit card earlier in the day by tricking their way into an office and removing cards from purses and wallets. They then called from outside the building, knowing where to call, and who to ask for from the names on the credit cards. So, armed with your cards and PIN they can freely spend and withdraw cash.

Vulnerability analysis

The fraud is quick and effective, requiring simple social engineering techniques to gain entry into the building and to construct a simple script as above. One additional benefit for the attacker is that the target doesn't report the loss of the card, as they assume it has been taken care of. Only days later, when the replacement card doesn't arrive, do they take any action, giving the fraudsters plenty of time to use the cards.

Possible countermeasures

- Better physical entry controls to work areas, and within areas better guidance to staff to keep personal items under lock and key.

- Better adherence to sound information security by the financial sector, such as avoiding the use of 'public' information to authenticate users and removing the communication channels that open the door to fraudsters.

- Building more effective security awareness for staff and customers so that fraud is more easily detected and dealt with.

- Banks really have to learn that most people do not understand the difference between the various elements of their digital identity. Some of the banks' typical authentication methods require you to tell them information that is semi-public, like your mother's maiden name. Other items such as your date of birth are very public. However, other items such as your PIN should not even be told to your bank. Can the average user really distinguish between something the bank requires you to tell them via a keypad, when you want cash (your PIN), and then expect you to understand never to give that information on the phone?

The above attack is effective and has some neat social engineering elements to it. However, you could argue that the risks of getting caught during an on-site attack are much higher, and therefore the gains should be greater than a small number of compromised accounts. So, let's return to our social engineering story and explore how an attacker can get some more substantial gains.

The Adventures of HackerZ – continued ...

If you remember, from the first instalment, HackerZ had conducted an attack on a 'software as a service' (to use the jargon) provider – CriticalX. By using some simple social engineering techniques, she was able to walk away with the entire Human Resources database for BankY – her ultimate target.

Following the successful attack, HackerZ was clever enough not to take the information and run. This may have alerted Johnny to the breach. If she suddenly disappeared he could start wondering about the last thing he did. HackerZ doesn't want any alarms being raised that get back to BankY. Instead, she continued to call Johnny on a number of occasions over the next few days and weeks. Eventually, she informed him that she was leaving the employment of BankY, thanking him for all his help.

She now returns to her primary target of BankY. She has two objectives in mind. Firstly, she would like to profit handsomely from her efforts. She doesn't agree with the typical hacker's aims of exploring systems for the challenge. She can think of many things to do with her ill-gotten gains. Secondly, BankY recently turned her down for a credit card, and she would get pleasure from seeing them suffer.

THE PRICE OF THE CARD

She has had some success with her hacking efforts so far. Ever the pragmatist, she finds the social engineering approach often to be the most efficient form of attack and seldom has to test her, somewhat considerable, technical abilities.

An area of particular interest to HackerZ is credit card data. This is a particularly attractive target as there is a ready market for the information. From one of her previous thefts, she has an existing buyer of data, who tells her that he has unlimited funds for full credit card authentication details. She is aware of the dangers, particularly as many 'buyers' are undercover law enforcement agents. She is avoiding the more public online stolen card market places such as Carder Planet and Carders Market, as she suspects these are actually being hosted by the law.

Her last sale was of 10 000 credit card numbers together with the card expiry dates. Although this is sufficient to generate card authorizations, she only managed to get $1 per number. Not bad for just a few days work. However, she is looking for a greater return with the potential risks she is taking. In addition, getting the funds through the complex money laundering route she has designed, to avoid tracing, is time consuming. This results in losing a percentage of the money. Another factor is that she doesn't use the same route twice, on the assumption that once used it must be compromised.

What she is really after is track data. This is the information recorded on the magnetic stripe on the reverse of the card. This includes all the information needed to clone the card, including such details as the three digit security code. This data is much more valuable. Her contact has offered her $20 per number and says he can deal with as many as she can find.

THE CHALLENGE – WHERE CAN YOU FIND CREDIT CARD TRACK DATA?

The obvious answer is by scanning a card, however single cards are not HackerZ's target. She wants a minimum of 50 000, as being a millionaire has its attractions. So she needs to find locations where this data resides.

The payment card industry is well aware of the threat. Their response has been to create the Payment Card Industry Security Standards Council. Their role is to develop and implement global systems of rigorous standards for organizations involved at all stages in the storage and transmission of card authentication details.

You may be thinking that 50 000 cards is quite a lot. However, in 2005, MasterCard International reported that 40 million credit card accounts (including Visa, Mastercard, American Express and Discover) had been 'exposed to fraud' through a breach at a payment processing company. It was announced that 68 000 cardholders were at 'higher levels of risk'. This breach involved placing some malicious code within the processor's network to extract information. This breach was made much more serious by the storage of security authorization codes, thus breaking the PCI standards. These codes should be deleted immediately after usage. This is the equivalent of the track data being targeted by HackerZ.

An interesting feature of breaches of credit card data is that the target organization cannot hide the incident in the same way as other information security incidents usually are. When card fraud happens it is possible to identify the 'common purchase point' by correlating the fraud to previous use of the cards. If all the cards in a given fraud had also used a common retail outlet, the source of the information leak is easily identified.

Fraudsters are learning this as it often leads to cards being cancelled before they have finished using them. Therefore, there are now instances where fraudsters will combine multiple sources of card data and rotate their usage. This is often combined with waiting up to 18 months from the original theft to the use of the card data. Another tactic to circumvent early detection.

BankY is an issuer of cards. This means that they offer a range of cards, both Mastercard and Visa. As the issuer, they ultimately receive the authorization requests and release funds. However, the high-volume transactions are across a reasonably well-secured network – the Payment Brand Network. HackerZ considers this too high a risk target and network compromises are not her strong point.

Her analysis has led her to an interesting organization – CardA. As with CriticalX, this organization routinely advertises on its website who its customers are. As a manufacturer of credit cards, CardA needs to receive, store and use the card track data – and plenty of it! A great way to find the required 50 000 cards, and hit BankY where it hurts.

CardA prides itself on its security. ID cards for employees and visitors, 24/7 security guards, CCTV, infra-red sensors and meticulous security and tracking around the cards during, and following, production. A great challenge for HackerZ.

An obvious route could be to go and work for CardA. However, an initial application resulted in indications that the identification checks on employees may cause a problem. Also, going to the lengths of working for someone is too time consuming, and HackerZ still has a day job to hold down until this particular hacking activity pays off.

So, how do you get access to the heart of CardA's operation, into the depths of their card data processing and the vital card track data? This looks like a job for a security auditor! CardA will be used to regular audits, perhaps a little too used to it. Perhaps even complacent.

HackerZ needs to assume the role of an auditor that will get special attention and privileged access. A Payment Card Industry special investigator should do the trick. HackerZ has no idea if this role is real. However, that is not important, as the objective here will be to get CardA to believe it. What better strategy than to get CardA to be introduced to the special investigator by their number one customer.

Stage one of the attack is to prepare the way for the visit of the special investigator. Armed with a wealth of HR information about BankY, that she obtained from CriticalX, HackerZ has mapped out the employee structure in the security-related departments. This was possible because the database had line managers indicated for each employee. Not only that, but she has additional information such as employment start date and salary information.

HackerZ's first step is to adopt the role of a new female administrator within the compliance department of BankY, and make the first contact with CardA.

CONTACT 1: MONDAY 11:00AM

HackerZ:	Hello, this is Debra Jennings from BankY. I wonder if you can help me?	*Comment: HackerZ has again adopted the new employee role to conveniently explain why she didn't have the right contact. In addition, HackerZ is using a slightly false accent (not her strong point). This is because later she plans to adopt the role of the special investigator to gain access, probably encountering some of the same people that Debra will have spoken to.*
Receptionist:	Yes, who would you like to speak with?	
HackerZ:	Well, I am new to BankY, but I need to speak to whoever looks after card security for us.	
Receptionist:	You probably want Miles Harrington-Brookes, he is our security manager. Would you like me to put you through?	
HackerZ:	Yes, thank you	
Miles:	Harrington-Brookes. (Assertive to point of aggression!)	*Comment: HackerZ is profiling Miles already (more on this in Section 2 of this book). His name gives clues to his background. His manner on the phone confirms this. He could be a risk, however he also may be useful during the attack.*
HackerZ:	Good morning Mr Harrington-Brookes, this is Debra Jennings, I work for Jessica Antle here at BankY.	
Miles:	Good morning Debra, how may I be of assistance?	

HackerZ:	Are you familiar with Jessica Antle's area?	*Comment: This is important to establish. If he was on first name terms with Jessica then he may make contact with her regarding this matter. HackerZ has chosen to use real contacts within BankY. An alternative strategy is to make them up. With a large financial institution people can be hard to identify. If an attacker uses fake identities, and only gives mobile contact numbers, this can be an effective way to avoid being found out.*
Miles:	No, never met Ms Antle.	
HackerZ:	Well Jessica heads up our regulatory compliance unit. She has asked me to call you regarding a PCI audit we are in the middle of here at BankY.	*Comment: HackerZ is reusing Sarah Clark as an identity. This has the advantage that, having used it a number of times before, she is more likely to react when, on-site, if someone says her name. The obvious disadvantage is that if she is ever discovered, the name could be recognized and circulated within the bank. She therefore decides that after this attack, Sarah Clark will be retiring, even if HackerZ continues on her chosen career path.*
Miles:	Oh. Yet another audit.	
HackerZ:	Yes, they are looking at our card holder data security. I understand you look after the physical security around our card manufacturing.	
Miles:	Yes that is right	
HackerZ:	Well next week we have an auditor with us, Sarah Clark, and she has asked if she can visit your facility. Sorry for the short notice, but would you be available to show her and myself around?	

Miles:	Nothing like giving us notice. I will need something in writing, but I could free up some time on Tuesday. Can you give me details of what she will be wanting? We are very busy here you know.	

This presents HackerZ with a challenge. Does 'writing' mean a quick email? This can be 'spoofed' easily so it looks like it comes from the bank. However, Miles is very likely to reply, and the reply would go to the bank.

An alternative would be to register a domain that looks very much like the bank's own domain. For example, bankycompliance.com is available to HackerZ. Very unlikely that Miles would notice the difference, especially as he is a physical security specialist, not an IT expert.

However, in this case, HackerZ decides to communicate in writing to give the maximum impact and sense of authenticity.

She decides to construct two letters. Firstly a letter from Jessica Antle to Miles, explaining the need for the audit. To this letter she decides to attach a copy of a letter from the special investigator, Sarah Clark, explaining the audit.

Letters need to be on headed paper, however this presents no particular challenge. Firstly, by its very nature, an organization's headed paper is distributed widely. Secondly, the free availability of desktop publishing software, and high-quality colour printers makes copying very easy. In the case of BankY, Sarah kept a copy of her credit card rejection letter, making the copying quite easy. She also designs a suitable Payment Card Industry Security Standards Council headed paper, following 5 minutes on the PCI website, where she finds a high-quality logo from a PDF document. A few more minutes searching and she actually locates a PDF of a letter from the Council posted on the Internet. Fifteen minutes later she has a suitable letterhead ready. This doesn't have to be of fantastic quality, as she intends to photocopy the final letter for attachment to the letter from Jessica to Miles.

So firstly the letter from Sarah (the special investigator) to Jessica Antle at BankY:

Jessica Antle
Head of Compliance
BankY

PCI – Issuer Investigations Unit Audit

Dear Jessica

Thank you for your time on the phone today.

To confirm our discussion, I shall be conducting a routine audit of your card issuing processes from Monday 6 August to Friday 10 August.

I will be calling you before then to discuss the likely coverage. However, you will understand that due to the nature of these audits, only a minimum amount of notice regarding scope is declared beforehand.

I look forward to speaking with you soon.

Yours sincerely

Sarah Clark
Special Investigator
PCI SSC

This is then printed, then photocopied and attached to the second letter from Jessica Antle to Miles:

Miles Harrington-Brookes
Security Manager
CardA

PCI Card Security Audit

Dear Miles

I understand from Debra Jennings that you have been informed of our imminent audit by the Payment Card Industry Security Standards Council.

As you understand, this audit extends to our suppliers involved in the card issuing process, and we have been informed by Sarah Clark, the special investigator, that she requires to spend a day with yourselves.

At this stage, we expect the visit to yourselves to be a walk-through of the physical security surrounding the card production process.

I have every confidence that your security will meet the expectations of the auditor.

Debra Jennings will be co-ordinating the activities on the day, and will be in touch to finalize the arrangements.

I thank you for your cooperation at short notice.

Yours sincerely

Jessica Antle
Head of Compliance

HackerZ keeps the letters short, as more detail may lead to mistakes. In addition, at this stage she isn't sure as to the knowledge that Miles could have of the Security Standards Council and its operations. She is relying on the short notice to ensure that he won't do any verification. Also, she is confident that the need to satisfy BankY, as a major customer of CardA, will be at the forefront of Miles's mind. The letters are just another piece of the jigsaw that reinforces the belief that this is genuine.

HackerZ sends the letter to Miles, and calls him promptly. This is to avoid Miles trying to call her, or even worse Jessica. This allows her to confirm times. She also gives Miles her mobile number (a phone bought for cash over the counter with pay-as-you-go credits – both purchased at some distance from HackerZ's residence).

The final stage of preparation is for HackerZ, as Debra Jennings, to give last minute apologies for the fact that she can't accompany Sarah on the day.

Now, one significant challenge presents itself during this preparation. Miles informs her that anyone visiting the site needs photo ID to get access to the building. This gives HackerZ two options:

1.   create some fake ID for Sarah Clark;

2.   use some social engineering to gain access without the ID.

She opts for the latter.

As the day of the audit approaches, HackerZ rehearses the audit, and her likely plan, in her mind. She isn't sure exactly how she will get hold of the card data, however she has some ideas. Her experience tells her that opportunities will arise once she has access to the site.

Dressed in her best business suit, she arrives by taxi 15 minutes before the allotted time. The security guards on the gate check her name against a list of visitors for the day and then the taxi is allowed to approach reception. She enters prepared to bypass the first security countermeasure.

HackerZ:	Good morning, I'm here to see Miles Harrington-Brookes.	*Comment: The receptionist checks her list. A good security feature, although you should ask yourself what happens if someone isn't on the list. Often there is no difference in how visitors are dealt with. The receptionist calls Miles and informs him of Sarah's arrival.*
Receptionist:	Thank you. Can I have your name please?	
HackerZ:	Sarah Clark. He should be expecting me.	
Receptionist:	Can I have your photo ID please?	*Comment: Using the name of BankY at this stage is deliberate. It is very unlikely that the receptionist has the authority or inclination to stop a BankY representative from gaining access. Are they going to force HackerZ to leave, and come back again with the right ID?*
HackerZ:	Photo ID? I haven't been told that I need photo ID.	
Receptionist:	I need photo ID to give you access to the site.	*Strict access systems usually have exceptions. HackerZ is going to be one of these exceptions. In addition, she is relying on the fact that Miles is in charge of security. He will be able to create exceptions.*
HackerZ:	Miles is expecting me. This has been arranged by BankY.	
Miles:	Good morning Sarah. Are you all signed in and badged up?	*Comment: Miles has the authority to do this, so he isn't breaking any (of his) rules.*
Receptionist:	She doesn't have any photo ID Mr Harrington-Brookes	

HackerZ: I should have been told about this. I am on a very tight schedule. I understand Debra's not here either. We have a lot to get through.

Miles: Yes, I can take responsibility for Ms Clark.

Receptionist: I just need to take your photo for your badge.

Comment: HackerZ had seen the small web camera on the reception desk. This didn't concern her. She knows from experience the extremely poor quality images produced and doesn't worry about leaving this behind after the attack.

Miles: I haven't been given a schedule, can you tell me what you need to see, and how long it will take?

Comment: HackerZ is using some authority here. She is deliberately changing the plan from Miles' suggestion. This is important as she wants to establish some compliance on his part as this is habit forming. She takes care to do this away from the receptionist. Miles is more likely to comply if he isn't doing it in front of a member of his team

HackerZ: Yes. You need to walk me through the security around the card authentication process. Depending upon what you show me, we can then look in more detail at other areas. This may take most of the day. I hope Debra warned you of that.

Miles:	Yes, that is fine. We'll start with the data centre.	
HackerZ:	Actually, I would like to start with your incoming communication lines, as I need to track the whole data path.	

HackerZ has prepared some audit documentation. This serves two purposes. Firstly it adds some more authenticity to the proceedings, building upon the established belief in her identity. Secondly, it adds weight to her questioning. As she fills in the documentation, the expectancy from Miles is that this process is required. The implication of each question is that this is part of the official process. You can get powerful results from a series of questions that the target sees written on a form.

Miles proceeds to show HackerZ the in-depth security features of the whole operation, staying with her at all times. He knows the systems well, and HackerZ can make a good assessment as to his competence. She recognizes that he isn't going to be easy to manipulate into giving her unnecessary access. She thought this may be the case, and decides to follow her backup plan. Just before lunch, she informs Miles:

HackerZ: Well Mr Harrington-Brooks, I can see that your physical security is very well developed. Apart from those minor issues with CCTV coverage we discussed at the rear of the building, I can see everything is in order. Now I need to examine the IT systems themselves.

Miles: Sorry, I thought this was just physical security.

HackerZ: No, didn't Debra make this clear? It is the whole security surrounding the credit card making process. If this isn't your area, then I will need someone from IT to help me.

HackerZ knew enough about the operations of CardA, and from her previous experience, to know that Miles wouldn't cover both physical and IT security.

She is deliberately giving Miles no warning as she wants this to be dropped on IT at extremely short notice.

The strategy works a treat. The IT department cannot easily refuse the request and has to allocate someone to help HackerZ. Young James Harding is duly produced, a second line support analyst. Miles hands over to James for the rest of the day. This handover allows HackerZ to establish instant belief in her identity from James, as she has been introduced on-site by the head of security.

HackerZ is also now within her comfort zone regarding the technology. Her expertise in physical security is not as good.

She is in luck in two capacities:

Firstly, James is only too happy to log into systems and show the inner workings. HackerZ establishes that this is the level of audit that she needs.

Secondly, he isn't very good at policing her. He gets bored quite quickly, and keeps popping out for a few minutes. HackerZ encourages this by making copious notes at various points, stopping conversation and leaving James as not a lot more than an observer.

In terms of the scope of a PCI audit, she quite rightly focuses on the card data, as delivered by BankY. The security of this data, before ultimately ending up printed on the credit card and written to the magnetic stripe, is crucial. Unlike merchants, who can greatly reduce their risk (and comply with the rules) by removing critical data from systems once payment authorization is received, card manufacturers need the data to make the card.

By the middle of the afternoon, HackerZ finds herself in the perfect position:

- sat in front of a PC, logged into James' administrator account;

- James has been called away;

- she is in an unsupervised area, with no visible CCTV coverage;

- she is looking at the card data, including the 'crown jewels' track data. The system in question is used for audit checks, so stores historic data of cards produced over a long period of time;

- James got to the data in such a way that she can see the underlying database files.

The actual attack takes a few seconds. Her mobile phone has all the data capacity she needs. A small USB adaptor cable is in her bag. The phone is connected to the PC, the data is copied across.

HackerZ continues with the 'audit' for another 2 hours before declaring that she is happy and makes her exit.

She couldn't wait to view the results. In the taxi leaving CardA, she connects the phone to her laptop (this had been kept by the front desk at CardA for good security reasons). A quick query of the data reveals 250 000 card details. That is about $5 million on the open market. An added bonus is that the details are for a number of card issuers, not just BankY. This could potentially make the tracking of fraud more complex, as the compromised cards will not have common points of purchase or issuer.

She now has to worry about the identity of her buyer. She suspects that a number of buyers are from the FBI. But that is another story ...

VULNERABILITY ANALYSIS

Manufacturing credit cards requires serious security measures. The motivation for an attacker is large and the potential payback huge. Therefore the time and effort likely to be put into an attack is substantial.

Detailed testing and analysis of security vulnerabilities is required. This should be combined with suitable risk assessments at each stage of the operation, with in-depth coordination between physical and IT security.

In this case weaknesses were evident right from the first call. The receptionist did not have to give out the name of the security manager and put the call through. BankY would know who to call and should have direct contact details. For communication with this key customer, a much better strategy is to:

- take the details of the enquiry;
- call a known contact within BankY, to confirm the details;
- call the person back.

Now this could appear to be a little inconvenient and time consuming. However, it demonstrates good security to existing customers and is acceptable if done efficiently.

The case of HackerZ demonstrates a fundamental weakness that we shall be exploring in more detail in Section 2. Our belief in identity is too easily established. There has not been proper verification of Sarah Clark at any stage. All the information flow has been one way – from the attacker to the target.

The reception requirement for photo ID is a good feature. In some cases this can be further strengthened by retaining the photo ID of the visitor during their visit. This greatly increases the chance of any access badges/cards being returned at the end of the day, as they will be swapped for the ID left earlier.

The photo quality of most reception systems is too poor to be effective. Many of these photos are no better than a silhouette. Both the quality of the camera and the lighting conditions around the desk combine to make these often not much better than CCTV quality.

Another factor here is the length of time that reception images are kept. It is important to remember that, in the case of credit card fraud, it could be many months before the data is used. Therefore, will the image data still be around in 12 months time to allow an identity match? This also assumes that a future forensic investigation, following detection of the fraud, will link the visit by Sarah Clark to the crime.

You should really examine the access you give to auditors. Do they really need all the access they ask for and expect? In addition, from most audits I have observed, you should ask yourself whether it is necessary for them to take any copies of documents?

HackerZ was able to change the nature of the audit, moving from physical security to IT security. The original request by Miles for information about the audit was refused on the basis that too much notice couldn't be given. However, CardA should, at a minimum, have clarified the areas to be seen and the people it needed to have available. This is a reasonable process that can be explained to the auditor as a requirement to ensure that the audit is effective.

The use of electronic equipment in secure areas should be examined in detail. The mobile phone is becoming a high-risk item for a number of reasons:

- Most phones now have inbuilt, relatively high-quality, cameras (often with enough resolution to copy documents).

- It can be compromised, turning the phone's microphone into a very effective listening bug. In some cases, this can be connected to remotely, via a second phone number, even when the phone is switched off.

- As in our example, it can be used to store increasingly large amounts of data.

- Although more in the arena of the security services, any device that emanates radiowaves, can be a concern in high-risk environments.

The final element of the attack had much greater impact, due to the large amount of historic data stored in this database. Data of this type should only be kept for as long as is absolutely necessary.

In addition, system designers have a habit of copying data for testing or auditing purposes. In many cases this doesn't present a risk. However, credit card data is particularly at risk and copies should be strictly controlled.

Clearly the last vulnerability was James' sloppy use of his administrator account, and leaving HackerZ unaccompanied. His belief in her identity was stronger than his security awareness. A feature of 'secure' operations is that employees often develop bad practices within these areas, on the false assumption that the bad guys are on the outside.

This example shows the potentially huge gains that can be achieved with social engineering techniques. This on-site attack showed nerve and cunning, yet didn't require very advanced techniques. Some meticulous research allowed HackerZ to be convincing, however, the actual final attack was easy. The countermeasures were not good enough to withstand a targeted attack such as this.

From my initial work with social engineering testing, and the subsequent development of protection systems, I have been fascinated with the psychology behind the human vulnerabilities we have been illustrating so far.

The development of all areas of technical information security attacks, from website hacking to wireless sniffing, shows us that as stronger protection is developed the attacks become more sophisticated in response. Therefore, I decided that we needed to develop a much better understanding of the nature of human vulnerabilities, so that we could not only defend against current attacks, but also predict future attack vectors.

The next section explores some important areas of this research. This knowledge has been extremely useful in conducting a range of social engineering testing programmes.

Understanding Human Vulnerabilities

Trust Me

A social engineer's primary goal is to develop the trust to enable them to carry out their attack. Therefore, it is essential that we thoroughly understand the processes that make up the development of trust.

For an organization to function effectively, it needs to store information between people in a variety of situations. However, in understanding and protecting ourselves from social engineering attacks, it is important that we understand where the limits of trust should lie. We shall also be showing just how flaky the foundations of trust can be and how easily it can be established with the target of a social engineering attack.

Trust is important to us, yet can also be very risky in certain situations.

The following example shows just how trusting people can be, even when the consequences are dangerous. It is an interesting example of how well-educated professionals can be made to undertake specific actions, against all their training and better judgement, if they accept the authority of the person who is telling them to do so.

Incident: Nurses Killing Patients

One well-known experiment was that conducted by Stanley Milgram in the 1960s and presented in *Obedience to Authority*, 1974. Milgram led the participants to believe that they were a part of a memory experiment; testing recall and that they, as the teacher, should punish the learner with electric shocks. The intensity of the shocks were increased as the learner (unseen, yet heard) got an increasing number of questions wrong. As the experiment proceeded the teacher continued to administer shocks, even when the apparent feedback (and latterly lack of feedback) indicated the learner was possibly dead.

It showed how the majority of a given population can be quickly manipulated into performing deadly actions on fellow human beings. It has been well documented, so I will not analyse it in depth here. However, it is still interesting, especially to challenge any mistaken beliefs that groups of people who commit atrocities are somehow different to the rest of us.

There is another interesting experiment that is worthy of examination. During the 1960s a group of researchers in the US were investigating cases where skilled nurses had not questioned doctors' judgement, even when the doctors were clearly making mistakes. The researchers conducted the following experiment:

A number of on-duty nurses were contacted by phone, by a man identifying himself as a doctor. In 22 cases the man instructed the nurse to give a drug to a specific patient on the ward. There were a number of good reasons why the nurses should have questioned the instruction:

- the drug was not authorized, nor on the stock list;

- the dosage instructed was twice the safe dose which was clearly stated on the container;

- a policy existed that stated prescriptions could not be authorized over the phone;

- the instruction came from someone the nurses had never met or spoken to previously.

Worryingly, only one nurse out of 22 refused to follow the instruction. You will be pleased to know that, as this was an experiment, the nurses who attempted to give the drug were intercepted.

Vulnerability analysis

These examples clearly show how people respond to authority. However, there are some interesting features. The 'success' rate is very high considering a) the professional status of the targets and their related training in patient care; and b) the single call.

In our experience, to get a hit rate this high you usually need to establish a relationship of some trust through a series of contacts.

So why did the nurses behave in this way?

Firstly, the notion that a nurse's role involves acting as a check and balance to the doctor is a complete fallacy. Nurses are trained from day one to follow doctors' instructions. In addition, questioning the doctor is not viewed as a good career move.

Secondly, is it likely that the nurse had ever encountered or been warned against this type of scenario? Almost certainly not.

Possible countermeasures

1. You should always be wary of any situation where authority figures can and do bypass procedure. It creates obvious vulnerabilities for the attacker to exploit.
2. Elements of peer review and segregation of duties can help here. If one nurse had to issue the drug, and another administer it, then you have two opportunities to question the instruction. Also, two people are more likely to challenge a request as they do not feel as isolated in the face of an authority figure.

However, given the mindset of the nurses demonstrated in this example, I believe that even this double check would not have guaranteed a refusal to comply. After all, both nurses would presumably have the same conditioned response to a doctor's request. Numerous previous instances of having to respond in an emergency, under pressure, will have effectively trained the nurses to follow instruction.

Trusting the Attacker

SENIOR MANAGERS WORKING AGAINST SECURITY

The above example illustrates the difficulty in developing an effective security culture where individuals are required to challenge authority figures. This is an important element to consider when building your social engineering protection. There are numerous cases of senior staff routinely bypassing security rules and procedures and expecting others to also do the same on their instruction.

You need strong backing from the people at the top of organizations to support security. This requires consistent activities to help senior managers understand the threats and potential impacts of information security breaches.

This task is getting easier as cases generate more publicity. A current example is the security breach involving the loss of millions of records of personal data by the Inland Revenue and Customs (the UK tax authority) which led to the head of that department resigning.

Events like this do help get the attention of senior managers. In general, the media attention is helpful in strengthening the case for increasing the effectiveness of information security countermeasures. However, in this case I wonder whether the immediate resignation of the head of the department was appropriate. In many cases there are two possibilities for the person at the top:

1. The incident was a genuine mistake, or intentional breach of policy/procedure. In these instances disciplinary measures, or extra training, is required at the level of the actual incident within the organization. It is not appropriate for the person at the top to resign.

2. The incident is associated with known weaknesses in information security that have previously been communicated to management, with no action taken. Or management had been made aware of the widespread weaknesses in information security and taken no action. In these instances it is appropriate for senior people to take responsibility.

In this particular incident, involving a government department, it is likely that someone had to do the 'honourable' thing. Pressure from the media will have played a big part in the response.

So senior managers have much responsibility, not only in leading the development of an information security programme, but also in demonstrating their commitment on a day-to-day basis by complying with policy and procedure.

THE POWER OF TRUST

The example of the nurses' compliance was partly due to the authority position of the doctor and also the natural tendency of the nurses to trust the identity of the person calling. This tendency to trust what people tell us is exploited time and time again by social engineers.

There are occasions when you cannot rely automatically on trust. Trust needs to be built up over time and there are gradations in the trust required depending upon the situation and risks. I suggest that you require one level of trust to lend someone £5 and rather more trust to let someone inject you with a drug (especially having read the example above).

Therefore, a social engineer needs to acquire the skills needed to develop trust with their target in proportion to the task they are going to request from that target. One attack could be easily accomplished in a single telephone call whilst another may take many weeks of developing trust, both off-site and on-site, to totally convince the target of the attacker's identity before the attack is effective.

Tricks to Building Rapport

If we want to develop trust with someone in order to deceive them into giving us information or performing an action, then developing rapid rapport can be key to our success.

Many observers have pointed to the fact that people in a high state of rapport will mirror each other's body language. You can see this when observing people in public, where couples who are attracted to each other will tend to be mirroring (that is, copying) each other's posture and movements. It is at times as if they are deliberately doing this and concentrating on it, however it is usually a completely subconscious activity.

This has been translated by some into the simple instruction to mirror someone's body language if you want to develop instant rapport. This can easily be detected. In logical terms the mistake is to observe that rapport leads to mirroring and therefore conclude that mirroring leads to rapport. This is not necessarily the case.

Rapport is actually developed following a complex mix of attributes which can convince us into feeling confidence and trust in someone, including:

- Dress – we tend to dress to project a certain image and to try and reflect something of our perceived personality. Therefore, someone dressing in a similar style to us is likely to be similar to us, and therefore more likeable.

- Looks – this is more than just being 'good looking', although that helps. When judging you for the first time, someone will tend to allow you to inherit the characteristics of the person/people that you remind them of. Our natural prejudice is a genetically inherited process, important to judge whether people we meet are a threat.

- Voice – especially the tone, and speed of speech. This is often an indication of the current state of mind, and a reflection of the communication mode the person is in at the time. This will be explored later when we look at Neuro-Linguistic Programming (NLP).

- What we actually say. After all, would you develop instant rapport with someone stating views that were the complete opposite to yours, even if they were sat in front of you mirroring your body language?

When teaching rapport building during one of my social engineering masterclasses, I often point people to a number of different techniques to develop rapport with ease.

Without these other factors, simple body language mirroring does not come across as genuine. It is in these situations that someone is more likely to detect that they are being manipulated in some way.

MIRRORING BREATHING

This technique can be powerful. Since a person's state of mind is reflected in their breathing rate, you can quite quickly begin to match them by mirroring this attribute. It is also difficult to detect, partly because the technique is not as well known as simple mirroring. Nevertheless, be careful not to stare intently at the person's chest as this can cause offence. Subtle movements of the shoulders are usually sufficient to pick up on the rate.

This approach to developing rapport has some added benefits. Firstly it helps you forget the body language mirroring, although you may naturally do this as you mirror their breathing. ('Natural' mirroring is generally a good thing, as it is unlikely to be misinterpreted as forced and artificial.) Secondly, it means you are likely to talk less, and follow the second point:

TRUE LISTENING

True listening is the sort of listening that people rarely do; an intense concentration on the content of what the person is saying. This will tend to have a powerful effect, particularly since it is quite a rare experience for most people. In conversation, most people are spending their time formulating what they want to say next; whilst not actually listening. The other person quickly picks up on this. The reason we don't object is that we are so used to this in many conversations. When the opposite happens, it can have a powerful effect upon us.

One great aid to listening intently is to try and repeat back portions of what the person is saying. Salespeople use this technique to encourage you to say 'yes'.

Say, for example, someone says to you, 'If we are really to establish a comprehensive information security management system, then we must give the appropriate attention to our human vulnerabilities'.

You can say, 'So if we are to really establish a comprehensive information security management system, then we must give the appropriate attention to our human vulnerabilities'.

They will then look at you as if you are rather strange. If you keep on just repeating back to them their words, they will either get bored with the conversation (or lack of), or think you are going slightly mad.

Remember, we are trying to show that we really are listening, and understanding, what they are saying to us. So let's rerun the example, and use a little more intelligence in our response.

The reply to, 'If we are to really establish to comprehensive information security management system, then we must give the appropriate attention to our human vulnerabilities,' could well be, 'I see, so we mustn't put all our efforts into just technical countermeasures?' 'Exactly!' could be their reply.

The 'I see' is expressing understanding. By saying that, you have not only listened, but also translated the idea into an internal picture. This is extremely powerful if the other person is primarily visual in their internal processing. More of this in the next chapter when we explore reading people in more depth.

The rest of your reply shows you have listened and understood. Rather than simple mimicking, you have restated their idea, paraphrasing what they have said, using different words.

THE MAGIC PAUSE

Try combining this technique with counting to three whenever they stop talking before you start to speak. If they don't start again, then it really is your turn to speak. This is especially important if you are about to put new ideas (yours) into the conversation, because you may well have been constructing what you are about to say at the expense of listening. This will be quite evident if you interrupt them before they have finished. This is really like saying, 'Shut up now, what I have to say is more important than what you are saying.' Not a good way of developing rapport.

In social engineering terms simple listening can be a very powerful tool for the attacker. As many people have not experienced someone taking this level of interest in what they say the effect can be profound. They can feel as though they have just met a true friend, in a very short space of time. In addition, an attack strategy based on making friends is difficult to counter. 'Be suspicious of anyone who appears nice to you' is not a realistic training approach.

MIND SCRIPT

An alternative to forced mirroring is to use a mind script – a simple technique that you can use to direct your thinking with some powerful results. You may remember it was used earlier to gain access to a bank's drinks reception. In this application we want the other person to feel that we like them. So a simple answer is to really believe you do like them – your body language and other subconscious signals will naturally follow. However skilled and knowledgeable we are in human communication, it is very difficult to consciously construct each aspect of our behaviour. This is especially the case if you want to maintain the performance for more than a few minutes. Your conscious brain just cannot keep control over all the aspects of our communication (verbal and non-verbal) for any length of time before the subconscious naturally takes over.

As we shall explore in Chapter 7, although the subconscious is very powerful, it is relatively easy to manipulate. If you tell yourself something in the right way, your subconscious will believe it and begin to act in new ways commensurate with the new belief. You then don't have to consciously control your every movement.

I once attended an extremely effective 'train the trainer' course, during which the trainer managed to captivate, entertain and inform approximately 200 people for the day without any visual aids. The trainer effectively supplemented the materials with great examples. He gave us a great tip for establishing the right 'atmosphere' at the start of the training.

As we all assembled in the room, he stood at the front, watching us taking our places, and making small comments and greetings, avoiding any lengthy conversations. He later told us he was making an effort to find something to like about every single person, even if it was only their choice of shoes. Notice he didn't concentrate on the shoes being nice, rather on thinking that the person was good for making such a wise choice. He was in fact running his own mind script to like the people he was going to train. He was setting himself up for a good day whilst his subconscious would be giving out all the right non-verbal signals to the audience that he really liked them.

On talking with him later I discovered that he was a trained courtroom lawyer who had been part of the support team for one of the top US defence lawyers. I wonder whether this technique was taught to him with respect to establishing rapport with jury members. If it wasn't, then it should be.

I AGREE

Simply agreeing with what the other person is saying helps to develop rapport. Obviously this can have its challenges if the other person is saying something very silly or in complete contrast to your deeply-felt beliefs. However, you can develop your skills in finding areas of common interest that you can agree on. In terms of conducting a social engineering attack, personal opinions can be instantly suspended. An attacker may wish to use a mind script to help develop the same beliefs and interests as the target.

It is fascinating how quickly people develop rapport when they discover that they come from the same town or region. The size of the area of significance appears to be proportional to the distance they are from home. If you are in the next county, then your home town is significant. If you are on the other side of the world then home is a bigger area.

This tendency links back to our genetic need to belong to tribal groups. We tend to pick groups on a short-term basis. For example, where I grew up in the heart of Yorkshire, England, there was significant local inter-village rivalry, sometimes friendly, and sometimes not (particularly with young men after an evening of alcohol). However, these rivalries were quickly forgotten in, for example, a Yorkshire versus Lancashire cricket match. This northern rivalry was also put to one side when a North versus South event occurred. This in turn would be replaced by national allegiances if we were against another country, whether in something as simple as a sporting event or more serious such as military conflict.

Looking for areas of common interest and associations is a good tactic to build rapport. Skilled social engineers will build up profiles of individuals, where hobbies and outside interests can be a powerful knowledge base. Sales people (often skilled in social engineering techniques) will use this information in order to develop effective relationships with their customers.

DRESS

When conducting face-to-face attacks, making your appearance similar to that of your target, or to fit with your adopted attack role is an important part of an attacker's armoury of techniques. Dress may be a simple, yet effective, change of appearance as it is relatively easy and generally inexpensive.

The dress strategy can be as simple as enabling an attacker to blend naturally into a given environment. A design agency or e-commerce company is unlikely to share the same dress code as a bank or law firm. A little target reconnaissance can go a long way in deciding what may be an appropriate dress for a given attack.

HAIR

Changing hair, either through restyling or with a wig, is another technique for the social engineer. Using this tactic allows an attacker to disguise their appearance during reconnaissance activities; particularly when surveying sites for future physical security breaches.

PUTTING IT ALL TOGETHER

By combining techniques, especially if the attacker can really believe that they are like the other person, an attack will be convincing. By not explicitly using conscious body language, yet adopting other techniques that develop deeper rapport, the attacker will find that any body language will automatically fall into place in a very realistic way.

Reading a Person

Mind Reading

Arguably, the ultimate goal in understanding how the human mind works is to be able to read someone's mind simply by looking into their face. Imagine if all your confidentiality countermeasures could be bypassed by someone who could just read the mind of a key employee. Let me give you an example:

When not busy solving information security challenges, I try to spend as much time as possible with my family. My wife, Ravinder, and our three children Alec, Oscar and Mia (13, 11 and 8 at the time of writing) love to play their 'family games'. One such game, you probably know it well, they call 'Guess Who'. Basically, you write the name of a famous person on a piece of paper, and stick it on someone's forehead – everyone else can see who you are except you. Taking it in turns you then ask simple yes/no questions until you find out your identity. For example:

'Am I male?' – Yes

'Am I a sportsman?' – Yes

'Do I play football?' – Yes

'Have I played for England' – Yes

'Is my name David Beckham?' – Yes

This is a simple, logical pathway to the answer. Of course sometimes, especially the younger members of the family, may miss out on the logical approach and simply start with, 'Am I the Queen?'. This can lead to rather long and drawn out games. Even more so when someone gives you a character from television that you have never heard of – as is often the case with myself.

On one particular occasion I was doing a poor job of guessing my character, having only gained the following knowledge: male, non-human, cartoon, non-Disney. Everyone else had quickly identified theirs and I was the last one. I suspected that the character could be someone that I had never heard of, so I suggested I read the mind of my daughter to get the answer.

I simply asked her to stand in front of me, looking straight into my eyes. I then asked her to repeat the words again and again in her head. Staring directly into her eyes, I looked deep in concentration, peering into the depths of her mind. I then asked her to shout the words at me (in her mind).

Declaring 'Scooby Doo' to the amazement of everyone, I, of course, was correct at the first attempt. Now, whilst not looking for a career as the next Derren Brown, it did look impressive. So how was it done?

Reading a person from simply looking at their face is quite fascinating. In the next chapter we shall be exploring the use of Neuro-Linguistic Programming (NLP) to give insight into a person's thought processes by looking at eye movements. You may also want to explore some of the work, by people such as Paul Ekman, into facial expressions and how to read emotions. However, my example involved the direct reading of words said by someone in their mind.

You may be thinking that I could detect slight mouth movements that gave away the words my daughter was saying in her mind, or perhaps my family had inadvertently dropped clues in the game and I already had guessed?

The answer is a little more straightforward, I cheated. I had simply removed the piece of paper, taken a look, and put it back in place whilst the others weren't looking. The whole mind reading aspect was just a simple hoax to entertain the family. Worth remembering, especially when seeing some seemingly amazing mind reading performances.

However, I was using some psychological insight, particularly into our perception of our visual environment and our ability to spot things like someone cheating in a game. Magicians will tell you that it is relatively easy to trick someone when one-to-one and close up. You can direct their attention, particularly by getting them to intensely concentrate on certain aspects of the trick, and by 'relaxing' their attention at key moments you can carry out the sleight of hand. Groups are more difficult, especially those people at the periphery whose attention you can't direct. This is even more the case with children, who don't yet have the same established patterns of behaviour and are therefore more likely to concentrate when you don't want them to.

So in my case I had simply anticipated that I would be the last one to guess my identity, and looked for the opportunity when the other four people in the room were concentrating on each other. I simply peeled off the paper, in front of them, using body movement at normal speed, with nothing to try and hide my actions. If I had tried to conceal my actions then the changes to my movements could have caught their attention. Magicians, particularly the latest mind reading variants, have developed this ability to perform a relatively straightforward trick then present the results back as an amazing feat of mind reading.

My simple cheat turned into an 'effective' mind reading demonstration, and it serves our purpose here of placing some boundaries on the ability of someone to read a person completely. It is worth remembering that many demonstrations of the impossible are likely to be just that. Many magicians, and other performers with an element of mind reading, are masters at social engineering; often persuading the audience that there was something more profound happening than the reality.

However, if you are going to develop effective social engineering protection systems, there is real value in furthering your understanding of how different individuals may react to a given situation.

Personality Profiling

In my consulting work I often find it valuable to profile particular populations in order to ascertain certain characteristics that may be common within certain employment groups, and that could be exploited by an attacker.

I have examined and used many profiling systems, including psychometric tools such as Myers-Briggs indicators. One of the dangers of such systems is that they can be overly complex in structure, with the outputs often expressed in a series of statements that you can easily agree with. Apologies to people heavily involved in this area if I haven't done it justice, however trying to use 16 personality types to analyse areas related to security doesn't lead to usable results.

However, I do often adopt a personality profiling system that maps neatly to social engineering vulnerabilities and is simple enough for a wide range of clients to understand and adopt for their own use. You may find something else that works for you, such as the Big Five (Openness, Conscientiousness, Extraversion, Agreeableness and Neuroticism – sometimes abbreviated to OCEAN), attributed to Goldberg in 1993, with its roots back to research conducted as early as the 1930s.

I find the most useful model to be a four quadrant variation, having its origins in the work by Marston in 1928, where Dominance, Influence, Steadiness and Compliance make up the DISC method, the method we also use to characterize personalities into four groups. The actual labels we shall be using were introduced to me by a great friend, master of the mind, and superb trainer, Lewis Pinder. You may find similar systems with labels such as Pragmatist, Extrovert, Carer, Professional, and so on. We express the four personalities as in Figure 6.1.

It is important to understand that we only use a model when it offers us something of value in our analysis. No model is the 'truth' giving a definitive understanding. If it is useful, we accept it until we find something better.

Also, I am a firm believer in the flexibility of the human mind and how our personalities can vary at different times, depending upon our environment. Therefore, when we classify people according to such profiles, we usually apply it to their dominant behaviour within the work environment, as this behaviour is usually most interesting in relation to the associated information security vulnerabilities.

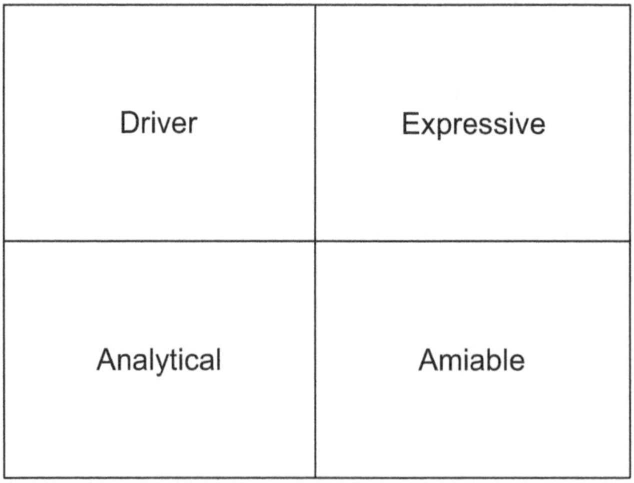

Driver	Expressive
Analytical	Amiable

Figure 6.1   Personality profiles

There are times when we want to focus on the behaviour of people outside the workplace. For example, we may be targeting people at home for a phishing attack or directing our efforts towards compromising home computers through the use of social engineering techniques. This can allow hacking back to the organization through the remote access Virtual Private Network (VPN) connections from the home computer. However, usually we are interested in protecting employees from attack in the workplace, therefore we take behaviour in this environment as the relevant point of analysis.

So we shall examine each of the personality traits in turn. It is useful for you to remember that at any one time a person may present a combination of traits. However, for the purposes of this introduction, we shall look at the more extremes of behaviour as described by the model.

DRIVER

A driver is primarily a results driven person, able to make quick decisions. They relish a challenge and can be very competitive. They tend to be good problem solvers and are effective in a crisis. However, their quick decisions can be just as quickly reversed if new information comes to light. They are self-reliant, extremely self-critical and can therefore appear direct and often forceful. Being risk takers, they are often adventurous.

EXPRESSIVE

You will find many expressive personalities working within the media and advertising, where their larger than life ego and entertaining side can flourish. They are sociable, generous and often charming. These people tend to have a strong focus on influencing other people, making a good impression to gain recognition and shaping their local environment. In general these people don't like too much detail and resist control in favour of expressing their own will. Their enthusiasm can also lead to impulsive behaviour.

AMIABLE

This personality is primarily focused on comfort, creating a stable and harmonious environment around them. They like predictable roles and a loyal group of friends. They tend to like one task at a time, with plenty of appreciation when it is done. They can appear rather passive, predictable and usually very calm.

ANALYTICAL

This person loves to concentrate on key details, thoroughly checking and weighing pros and cons. They like to analyse, adding structure through finding more information. They can take an age to make a decision as they need to find all the relevant information prior to being able to decide. However once a decision is made they will stick to it, as they must have taken everything into account in getting to that point. They apply the highest standards, with systematic approaches that can be bordering on being an absolute perfectionist.

USING PERSONALITY PROFILES

In general, most applications of similar personality profiling seeks either to help people develop more complementary skills or assist in helping people formulate teams, with an appropriate mix of approaches to particular projects. For example, you could say that pairing an Analytical with a Driver would be a good partnership in a managerial role. Of course, we are more interested in understanding how people can be manipulated and which techniques to focus on when analysing social engineering attacks and preparing defences against them.

By understanding the typical profile of people in different roles within the organization, we can begin to predict their behaviour when presented with different scenarios. For example, why would an attacker target management or the helpdesk rather than the sales team? This may well be the information they have access to or their predicted reaction to a given attack technique. For example, the risk taking, adventurous nature of a manager (Driver) may lead to them acting quickly when given an opportunity.

The personalities, driving forces and typical roles can be summarized in Figure 6.2.

MAPPING YOUR ORGANIZATION

From the analysis above, and my experience of applying this model, we can map some example profiles for different roles within a typical organization, as seen in Figure 6.3.

Now clearly, not everyone in each group will fit the profile, and you can see that groups are represented by a spread across the profiles. However, this type of analysis can be helpful in understanding how each group may be targeted with social engineering.

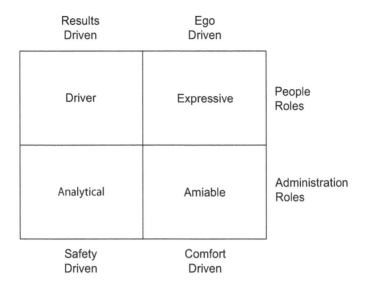

Figure 6.2   Personality profile driving forces and roles

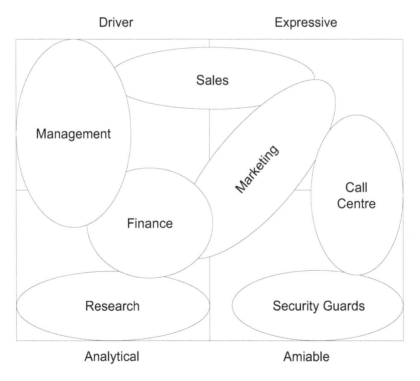

Figure 6.3   Typical departments mapped to personality profiles

TARGETING

When attacking an organization, an attacker may have specific target information or systems. However, often the attack vectors may be chosen on specific vulnerabilities or preferred routes. This is because, internal controls may be weak and therefore any route in can be used to get to the relevant target information.

So we shall examine two groups and see how the use of personality profiling can guide us in choice of technique.

Security guards

These are often extreme Amiable personalities. This may be a coping technique for their jobs where there is often long hours of boredom, with little physical or mental activity. Alternatively, it may be that the role is attracting certain personality types. As passive, and often predictable, individuals they are also prone to manipulation by anyone they feel to be in a management position. So an attacker may choose to adopt a management role and approach them as a figure of authority. However, more subtle approaches may have even better results: this could be to socially engineer them through giving the appearance that the attack is within existing rules and normal behaviour, as in the example below.

Incident: Hosting Equipment Thieves

As we are all increasingly dependent upon IT and network infrastructure, many organizations have chosen to outsource their hosting, moving their equipment to a 'secure' data centre. It has therefore shocked many hosting customers to learn of a series of incidents in which data centres have been targeted by people to steal equipment.

In one incident in late 2006 in London, thieves drove a van to the loading bay of an IT facility, loaded the van with equipment and drove away with a reported £6 million of equipment. The equipment in question was live at the time and needed unplugging and dismantling from racks. This affected numerous companies hosted within the centre, and in some cases led to disruption of many days.

Amazingly, they were watched by two security guards, one via CCTV and the other in person doing his rounds.

So why didn't the security guards challenge the thieves? According to news reports, the thieves had valid swipe cards to access the area in question, and therefore looked legitimate.

Vulnerability analysis

In our experience, too many IT data centres are focusing on security that sells services rather than real security. Incidents such as this are therefore easier to perform than you may expect.

The challenge in a facility such as this is the number of customers who need access, the regularity of equipment being delivered (and removed), and the low levels of staffing required to remain competitive. Therefore systems need to be especially effective.

Too often, we are shown expensive (often biometric) entry systems, only to find literal 'back doors' that are used by employees, contractors, and 'trusted' customers.

Possible countermeasures

1. Consider just how secure your swipe access systems are, in terms of card control, and the number of cards issued that can gain this sort of access. It is surprising how many organizations don't control their cards and do not promptly disable cards that 'go missing'.
2. A more comprehensive change control system with authorization levels would help here. A swipe access may be appropriate for accessing an area, however, is it really appropriate for removing equipment out-of-hours? Many such facilities require pre-booking for access; it is at this point that the nature of the visit can be ascertained. If this is going to involve removal of equipment, then a check can be made to an alternative contact within the requesting organization to verify the request.
3. Employ 'better' security guards, and test them periodically. A simple strategy is to take the best 10 per cent of the guards and train them to be testers, constantly looking for weaknesses and trying to exploit them. Then the remaining guards have to operate at more of a conscious level, as they never know if they are being tested. The results can be so dramatic that you don't need as many guards – therefore saving money.

Sales people

Individuals in a sales role are often extreme Expressive personalities, as sales is primarily a relationship building role. As with the security guards, people can be self-selecting in terms of personality.

An attacker may seek to appeal to the strong ego of the sales person, always looking for a quick win, and to look good in front of others. Most organizations put these individuals under pressure to deliver results. Often they have one of the only roles within an organization that have a direct pay relationship to their performance on a month-by-month basis, through the use of sales commissions. Therefore, they have very strong incentives related to delivering sales targets. Their natural tendency to be trusting, combined with the relative 'blindness' that can be induced by the prospect of personal gain, can be exploited to create a rapid relationship. They also have an understandable 'customer is always right' approach that includes supplying all the information that a customer needs to help them reach the right buying decision.

As sales people they will often leak critical information if they feel it will strengthen their relationship with a prospect and bring them closer to a sale.

Managers may also be targeted through their predictable behaviour:

Incident: Target Eye Limited

Target Eye was a software development company based in London, run by an Israeli husband and wife. The organization developed a trojan, used to infect a computer, spy on the user and steal files. They apparently first developed the software with the intention of selling it. However, when that didn't work they decided to make their own malicious use of the software, to spy on executives.

They targeted senior executives with a story of a lucrative business deal. Initially telephone contact was made and this was followed by an offer to send the target more information on a CD. Of course, given the nature of the business opportunity, the contents were sensitive and therefore should only be handled by the executive in person.

Upon arrival the executive would insert the CD, allowing the trojan to infect their PC, giving the attackers the access they needed.

Vulnerability analysis

This attack works well with executives, as the Driver side of their personality is interested in the rapid results and they will be eager to see the key points in the supposed business plan.

It is possible that the organizations in question had procedures for accepting information on CD, and perhaps a method of checking such media for malicious software. One potential issue here is that procedures for scanning media often involve executives having to take material to very junior helpdesk staff.

Remember a Driver certainly won't have the attention to detail to follow a procedure such as this and will not like having to ask for help from the helpdesk.

Possible countermeasures

1. Establish sound procedures for accepting data on a variety of media. When the only method was floppy disks, many organizations had tight procedures for virus scanning inbound disks – these have been relaxed with the proliferation of transfer media.
2. Get the backing of executives to follow the procedures – at all times.
3. Raise awareness amongst managers as to this type of approach that could target them.
4. Effective protective monitoring, to increase the chances of similar incidents being detected. The software in question would have to send its communication out of the organization through a network route, and therefore could be detected.

In addition, in some cases there is a sound case for developing specific information systems dedicated to the senior executives, with trusted senior IT staff given direct responsibility for their administration.

COLD READING

As we are looking at the area of personality profiling, it is useful to take a sideways glance into 'Cold Reading'. This term can be applied to a wide range of techniques, commonly deployed by a range of individuals such as psychics, mediums, palm readers and so on.

Cold reading is of interest on a number of different levels. Firstly, it is a good example of how people can be manipulated, specifically into believing something relates very personally to them, when actually the opposite is the case. It also illustrates our strong belief in our individuality when evidence points to us being much more alike in our behaviour.

I often apply a few of the common cold reading techniques in the social engineering masterclass that I deliver periodically. I present this to each delegate on the morning of the second day. Having had a day to interact with them, I give them a suitable introduction saying that I have used the information from the first day to construct an individual profile. During this introduction I am setting them up for the exercise and directing their expectations and interest. Given the previous content on profiling individuals they are expecting content based on profiling information.

Cold reading provides a useful contrast to profiling, an overemphasis on which can start to give people a false impression of the differences between individuals. This is especially true of profiling systems that use a wide range of different categories.

It is also worth noting that the results of some profiling activities are often presented with elements of cold reading techniques, with plenty of ambiguous statements that can be interpreted by everyone as relating to them.

I ask the delegates to read through their profile, and score it according to the level of accuracy to their personality. I also ask them, at this point, not to share the contents with the other delegates. This is essential, given that each profile is identical and the aim of the exercise is to trick them into believing that it has been written specifically for them.

In a recent case, one person declared it to be an 'amazing insight' into their mind. In fact, the person explained that they had recently had an in-depth psychological assessment over many days and this profile was more accurate. They declared their amazement at how accurate I could be after only a few hours of interaction with the group. I had to be careful not to allow the person to go too far as the risk of embarrassment after the 'reveal' was growing.

Below is a sample text. As you have not been 'primed', and are probably (having purchased this book), a sharp, analytically minded individual, I wouldn't expect you to be caught out by its trickery. The techniques, and some of the words used, are taken from Ian Rowland's excellent, authoritative work in this area. Please see the Further Reading for details of his work.

Personal Profile

Delegate Name Inserted

Career You can be a great business person, artist or parent. Creativity is a strong point and is likely to show itself in many forms. You can think and express yourself visually. Then again, you can express yourself in more subtle ways. You do have a tendency to take time over difficult decisions before you can take action. Although you are interested in personal wealth, you do not see wealth in purely financial terms. You are neither governed by money or a slave to it.

You enjoy learning, so long as you can see a tangible benefit, and practical applications for the knowledge. You can apply your creativity to solve problems. This makes for a very effective combination – a good learner and thinker. Therefore, you can be relied upon by your colleagues when it matters most.

You like to feel you are the architect of your own future and you have a healthy sense of responsibility for your own actions.

Relationships You can take a knock to your own pride or confidence, because you trust yourself to recover. But woe betide anyone who hurts or damages those whom you care for. You are a protector and a carer. You never, ever, forget an enemy whom you perceive to have injured someone close to you. Nor do you forgive yourself for having allowed your protective skills to have been thwarted.

You sometimes feel strong and can take on the chin some knocks that would send others down for the count, however, there are significant times when someone does manage to hurt you. When this happens you are sometimes stunned that your defences failed you. Moreover, you

> can be very effective at making your distress known to those around you.
>
> You are a great conversationalist, providing that you find someone with whom you share a common understanding and outlook on life.

Analysis

Let's look at this profile in some detail, examining the statements and the underlying techniques deployed.

Delegate Name Inserted	Using the name is important, as it adds to the belief that this profile is uniquely theirs.
Career *You can be a good business person, artist or parent.*	Given that the delegates are from business and 'can be' doesn't mean 'already are' this is a safe start. Artist or parents are also quite contrasting roles, so there is something for everyone. Given the typical age of the delegates, many will be parents, and how many parents would not like to think of themselves as good?
Creativity is your strong point, and is likely to show itself in many forms.	Most people wouldn't want to think they are not creative, and 'manifest itself in many forms' gives those who aren't very creative the opportunity to think more widely for examples that relate to them.
You can think, and express yourself, visually. Then again, you can express yourself in more subtle ways.	As most people have a strong visual focus this is quite a safe statement. However, it is also extended in a way that non-visual people can also agree with.

You do have a tendency to take time over difficult decisions before you can take action.

Surely the definition of 'difficult' is a decision that needs time thinking over? Therefore this is likely to be true.

Although you are interested in personal wealth, you do not see wealth in purely financial terms. You are neither governed by money or a slave to it.

How many people are not interested in their personal wealth? The following statements are to appeal to a person's natural tendency to want to believe that they are not completely consumed with making money.

You enjoy learning, so long as you can see a tangible benefit and practical applications for the knowledge.

A simple 'yes' from those who like learning, the rest is for those who are more critical – something for everyone. Also, it is not that profound to say that someone who has booked on a course to learn something new enjoys learning!

You can apply your creativity to solve problems. This makes for a very effective combination – a good learner and thinker.

This is purely complimentary. People usually agree with compliments.

Therefore, you can be relied upon by your colleagues when it matters most.

How many people can't be relied on 'when it matters most'.

You like to feel you are the architect of your own future and you have a healthy sense of responsibility for your own actions.

Most people would like to feel this.

Relationships

You can take a knock to your own pride or confidence because you trust yourself to recover. But woe betide anyone who hurts or damages those whom you care for. You are a protector and a carer. You never, ever, forget an enemy whom you perceive to have injured someone close to you. Nor do you forgive yourself for having allowed your protective skills to have been thwarted.

This hooks into natural tendencies for people to take revenge and makes it easier to agree with if the attack had been against someone else.

You sometimes feel strong, and can take on the chin some knocks that would send others down for the count, however, there are significant times when someone does manage to hurt you.

Everyone can think of when they feel strong, and also when they have been hurt. Giving generalities that the reader can tag to specific instances is very powerful. On later recollection, the 'victim' will often cite that the writer cited specifics that were actually only added by the reader's interpretation.

When this happens you are sometimes stunned that your defences failed you. Moreover, you can be very effective at making your distress known to those around you.

Using 'sometimes' allows for those times when it doesn't apply and invites the reader to think of the times when it does apply. There are times when everyone makes their distress known, if someone does this regularly they are likely to be amazed at the insight of this statement. If not, they can probably think of at least one occasion with which to agree.

You are a great conversationalist, providing that you find someone with whom you share a common understanding and outlook on life.	I particularly like this one, and so use it as a strong finish. A great conversationalist instantly says yes, and doesn't read the rest. Someone who isn't hooks on to the second half. This is another way of saying, 'You find it easy to talk with someone that you find it easy to talk with.'

The key here is to build the readers' expectations and then deliver a profile that they can say yes to. The more they believe, the more selective they will be in their interpretation, hooking into things of particular relevance and conveniently giving less weight to inaccuracies. They will also tend to add detail where none exists, especially if allowed time to expand their belief and modify their recollections following the reading.

Mediums

You can do some very interesting cold reading analysis for any televised shows in which mediums offer 'messages' from the dead. Their general strategy is to:

- Mention something general enough that someone in the audience will make a connection. For example, 'I hear a name starting with a J, and feel some problems in the chest area'. When someone offers 'that must be Jack, he passed on following heart problems', the medium can confirm this information.

- Introduce an element such as 'I see a dog as being important'. If this is a hit, then great, if not known it is likely another 'J' with chest problems and with a dog association is in the room.

Very little additional information is actually given, yet the recollections of the 'target' are often very different from the actual dialogue.

The example above would often be 'remembered' as 'he knew about Jack and his heart problems, and knew that he was so attached to that dog'.

Clearly the beliefs of the audience are playing a big part. I am often impressed with the medium's technique and the results on the audience, however, not with the information 'communicated' by the dead.

Signs to look out for are:

Names beginning with ...	(usually the most common letters)
Problems in the chest area ...	(accounts for 90 per cent + of deaths)
Man in a uniform ...	(most old people will have served in the military)
Common pets ...	(easy hits with so many pet owners)

Remember, the use of a reasonable-sized audience give very high percentage chances of success. And the difficulty of receiving communication 'from the other side' gives a good excuse if something isn't accurate.

I will be impressed when a medium says:

'I hear from a Wilbur, who died of a freak fingernail injury, and misses his pet ferret called Arthur. He has a message for Florence.'

Using these techniques

An attacker can use similar techniques as those used by mediums, at a more micro level, during rapport building.

General statements that are easy to agree with, and are subject to individual interpretation, can make the other person feel they have something in common with you, for example:

- 'You understand the challenges we face'
- 'Clearly we have to improve the situation'
- 'Things are not how they used to be'

The missing detail is added by the person hearing the message and is almost always guaranteed to get a 'yes' inside the mind of the listener. You can strengthen the effect by nodding as you say the words. This can be used to strengthen rapport.

Subconscious Mind

Neuro-Linguistic Programming (NLP) Profiling

Part of the foundation of Neuro-Linguistic Programming (NLP), established by Richard Bandler and John Grinder, was the formulation of theories of internal representations within the brain and the work of the subconscious.

An interesting part of this work was the use of observed eye movements to give an indication as to the working of the mind. These movements are rarely noticed by the observer until they are alerted to their presence. Not everyone exhibits the same movements and they are often reversed for left-handed people.

You can check them by correlating what someone is describing compared with their eye movements. For example, looking up and to your left is common when you are remembering a visual memory. So if you ask someone to describe the outside of their house, and watch the eye movements, you can confirm that this is the case for them. The memory processes indicated by specific short-term eye movements are shown in Figure 7.1.

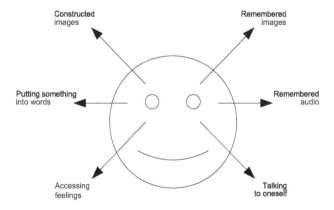

Figure 7.1   NLP eye movement reading

Moving around the circle, starting from the top right:

- Remembered images – these are visual memories being accessed during thought processes.

- Remembered audio – recollections of sounds or someone's words.

- Talking to oneself – this is an indication that an internal dialogue is in progress.

- Accessing feelings – people feeling depressed spend much time down here. This is one reason why it is often extremely difficult to feel sad whilst looking up.

- Putting something into words – in some cases this will be rehearsing something before it is actually said.

- Constructing images – making something up.

MIND READING

This works in a powerful way, in giving you clues to someone's thought process. For example, if you can spot the difference between remembered and constructed images, you can tell if someone is lying with a reasonable degree of accuracy.

You can also demonstrate interesting effects. For example, if you try to get someone to remember something visual and make them look down whilst they are doing so, they will find it almost impossible. The eye movements are not just indicators, they are also often essential to access the memory.

These observations can also enable you to identify someone's primary thinking and communicating modes. These are usually either visual, auditory or kinaesthetic (touch), with the majority of people very strongly visual.

There are other subtle variations that you can move on to as you develop your ability to read eye movements. For example, some people access visual memory by looking straight ahead, defocusing their vision. You can also notice other areas that correlate with communication mode, including posture and voice tempo and pitch.

Development of skills in reading these signals can be important in face-to-face social engineering, however, many attacks are conducted at a distance. You can get similar clues to someone's primary communication method in the words that they use; either verbally or written. The framing words used around key messages often contain the clues to the person's thought processes.

For example, when faced with the same problem, one person may say 'let's take a look', another saying 'lets' talk it through'. The first tackles problems visually, whilst the second addresses problems in an auditory way. Other examples include:

- 'shine the torch on this issue' – visual

- 'he seems to be blind to the problem' – visual

- 'I hear what you say' – auditory

- 'sounds good to me' – auditory

- 'I need to balance the issues' – kinaesthetic

- 'let's get a firm handle on this tough problem' – kinaesthetic

You can increase your persuasive skills considerably by mirroring the other person's mode of communication and therefore their thinking patterns.

Understanding the Subconscious

If we are to fully understand the way a person responds to a social engineer, it is important that we explore the subconscious mind. In this chapter we have used some NLP techniques to help understand an individual's primary communication system(s). It is worth looking back at the foundation of NLP, as it was originally conceived through extensive study of a renowned hypnotherapist, Milton H. Erickson.

Hypnosis provides many clues as to the way the human brain works, particularly in its decision making. Remember, the social engineer needs the target to assist in the attack in some way. This requires direction or misdirection and manipulation of the target into a decision and subsequent action that helps the attacker.

In this context we are not talking about stage hypnosis which is a special case of behaviour; a combination of individuals' expectations and special selection exercises (very rarely shown on any final TV broadcast) by the stage hypnotist.

Contrary to stage hypnosis, the field of hypnotherapy has much to offer in understanding the relationship between the conscious and subconscious mind. As with other concepts and theories throughout this book, we are selecting ideas that are useful in understanding social engineering and the development of countermeasures.

There are aspects to the relationship between the conscious and subconscious mind that some people find uncomfortable, yet this area of study has much to offer in our exploration of better understanding.

The first element of the relationship between conscious and subconscious is the significant power of the subconscious mind. Our subconscious can process vast amounts of information quickly and can multi-task. Take the example of learning to drive. When you first start it is a struggle to operate all the controls and observe the road ahead. As it is a new activity you are consciously trying to do too many things simultaneously: steer, change gear, accelerate, break, press the clutch and operate numerous hand controls. It is accepted that anything above four activities is a struggle for the conscious brain. From the above you can see that no conscious brain power is left to observe the multitude of things happening outside of the vehicle. No wonder it is stressful.

However, as you develop driving experience, you begin to feel more comfortable; some of the activities are moving into your subconscious where multi-tasking is easy. For example, you will press the clutch and change gear based on engine noise without (consciously) thinking about it.

The more you drive the more the whole activity becomes subconscious, even down to following the curve of the road, keeping up with the car in front and responding to red lights. For journeys that you know well, such as the commute to work, this can be dangerous. You will have experienced the sudden realization that you can't remember driving the last mile or two. Your whole driving experience has dropped into the subconscious and you have either been thinking of something else or moved into a light hypnotic state with restricted conscious awareness.

This process of turning a regular activity of driving a car into a subconscious activity has some interesting side effects. As we become over familiar with the layout of roads, junctions, traffic lights and so on, we tend to become over-confident. This effect has been studied, along with the effect of increased safety measures such as anti-lock brakes, leading to people driving in an increasingly reckless manner.

Interesting experiments, such as the Dutch 'naked streets', involve removing all road signs and markings. The effect, with no visual and subconscious clues, makes drivers concentrate consciously on their driving, with a subsequent decrease in accident rates.

It is interesting to examine other areas where the subconscious can influence. One subtle way is our hidden prejudices related to names. It is reasonably well established that we like people who we perceive to be like us. However, this has been found to extend to preferences related to our names. As described in *'YES! – 50 Secrets from the Science of Persuasion'* by Goldstein, Martin and Cialdini, it has been shown that people have small (yet statistically significant) biases towards choices that relate to their name. It has been shown that career choice shows a small bias that reflects this. For example, Americans called Dennis are 82 per cent more likely to be dentists than people with similarly common names. Also, people with names starting Geo (Geoff for example) are more likely to be geologists than others.

This name bias extends to people called Louise being slightly (just) more likely to move to Louisiana than people with unrelated names.

The social engineering attacker can use this bias as another small factor in increasing the likelihood that someone will like (and trust them). Calling someone, and having the same (or similar sounding) name is more probably going to lead to them liking you.

This subconscious bias has also been shown to extend to numbers. Towns with a number in the name (such as Three Forks, Montana) were shown by the same researchers to have disproportionate numbers of people with birthdays on 3/3 (3rd of March).

Now does this mean that you should be wary of employing anyone with names beginning with 'HA' in case they turn out to be HAckers? Clearly not, although I do know an information security manager called Mr Hackworth! It could make the choice of some names in children's books, such as Fred the Fireman, or Pat the Postman, seem rather interesting.

Remember this effect is quite small. It points to decision making being influenced by a variety of information in the subconscious in ways that we are not consciously aware of. The extent of this influence is something we shall be coming back to.

How do the conscious and subconscious minds interact? Firstly, the subconscious mind receives all of its input via the conscious brain. Your five senses are filtered through your conscious mind. Your subconscious 'view' of the world is a mixture of these senses and learned (or programmed) behaviour in response. You will have experienced how a given sense, a distinct smell is a good example, can trigger off the feelings and associated memories of past events. In some cases, things you consciously thought you had forgotten.

Figure 7.2 illustrates the relationship between the conscious and subconscious mind.

The proportions in the diagram are inaccurate – the subconscious brain is even larger and more powerful than this diagram depicts.

Another, very powerful, example of the power of the subconscious is illustrated by the experiments conducted by Milton H. Erickson and Linn Cooper in the 1950s. They were exploring time distortion.

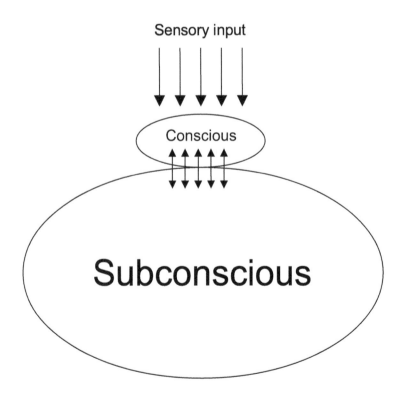

Figure 7.2   Conscious–subconscious brain relationship

One form of time distortion can be used to change our perception of time. I use this, for example, when driving. A feat easily accomplished with self-hypnosis to alter your experience, and recollection, of the passage of time. This utilizes our different perceptions of time, often dependent upon whether we are enjoying a particular activity. For example, you will have experienced waiting in a queue for what seems like an age, even though the actual time elapsed is often quite short. In contrast, you will probably have had fantastic holidays that seemed to flash past in an instant. Our perception of time is not constant and, therefore, is open to manipulation. You can change your perception of time in a given instance.

I make use of the technique to help me drive long distances between clients, without any frustration, arriving fresh and with a recollection of only a fraction of the time that has actually elapsed. As an example, a 4-hour drive will typically only feel like about 40 minutes. There are occasions when I have alarmed certain colleagues by explaining that I use hypnosis when driving. However, this is not entering a hypnotic trance state during driving, rather the use of self-hypnosis to condition one's brain prior to driving. In addition, during the self-hypnosis session, I also reinforce that I remain awake and alert during driving.

Depending upon how effective you are at the technique the effect can last for a considerable amount of time. Personally, when I first tried the technique it lasted about a year before I needed to 'top it up' with another session. By then I had improved my self-hypnosis and it hasn't needed to be repeated since.

Erickson's experiments explored a profound area, giving us insight into the power of the subconscious. You may have glimpsed the phenomena that Erickson was researching early in the morning as you are just waking up. You look at your clock, go back to sleep and dream for what appears to be 30 minutes, only to wake and discover that barely 5 minutes has passed. Your sleeping time perception is not the same as that of your waking time. Dreams appear to be much longer than they are in reality. Dreaming usually occurs late in the sleep cycle and may only last for a short period of time. Your recollection is that much more time has passed as you dreamt.

Erickson and Cooper took their observations further from 1948 to 1950, undertaking over 800 hours of experimentation. They trained subjects to enter hypnosis and use their 'special time' to undertake activities subconsciously. They then directed them to further activities that could be measured in terms of reasonable time to complete.

One technique they used was to have a constant sound source, such as a slow metronome, in the background during hypnosis. Then suggestions were made to the subject that the metronome was slowing down. In reality, it was the subject's perception of time that was expanding (or contracting, depending upon your point of view).

Other training techniques they used included repeatedly practising the same activity under hypnosis, allowing the subject to feel they had plenty of time. Example activities included doing regular household tasks, eating a meal, shaving, sewing, and so on.

In one, quite astounding, example a subject did the following in his 'special time':

- he was sitting alongside a swimming pool, in a swim suit;

- taking small lead shot from a bucket, one at a time, he counted them into another bucket;

- After counting 2 000 he would swim the length of the pool;

- He would then resume counting, although he reported difficulty after each swim due to his wet hands.

In total, before being brought back out of hypnosis, the subject counted 9 800 lead shot. When asked to show the rate at which he was counting, the rate was measured at 72 shot per minute.

Now, if my mathematics is correct, and I do have two A-levels in mathematics, then, without allowing time for the swims, I think about 2 hours, 16 minutes and 6.67 seconds (please excuse my rounding up for simplicity) should have been sufficient time.

Astonishingly, the actual real time taken was 5 seconds. By the end of the experiments it was routine for activities of approximately an hour to be completed in less than 10 seconds.

Another, perhaps more practical and useful, example saw a concert violinist using the same technique to rehearse lengthy pieces of music prior to performance. It took the violinist only seconds to practice long recitals, reporting that it 'helped my finger memory ... picking hard passages and playing them in several ways to facilitate speed and accuracy'.

You would be right to question this amazing feat. After all, how did Erickson know that the subject was not lying or hallucinating? I urge you to seek out the excellent book detailing these experiments. You will be impressed by the scientific rigour applied and the range of tests to check the validity of the results. However, some interesting tests were conducted by Erickson and Cooper that offered strong verification that the subject really had experienced the activity.

These tests utilized sound signals during the hypnosis session. Sounds were made during the hypnosis session and then the subject was asked to feedback on any sounds that they had heard during the activity. Remember that the subject is experiencing an activity over, say, 1 hour, whereas the sounds (in 'real' time) were at specific points during a period of, say, 10 seconds.

The sound used was a short sharp sound by striking a glass with a metal knife. Interestingly, the reported sounds from the person in hypnotic state were often interpreted in context of the activity they were experiencing. For example, the table below shows some activities and the reported sound.

Activity	Reported Sound
Baking a cake	Horn from a passing car outside
Picking flowers	Bird singing
Picnic	Train

The significant result, however, was the accuracy to which the subject could report the sound in relation to the time of the activity. If, in a 10-second session, the sound was created after 3 seconds, the subject would report it occurring between 15 and 20 minutes into their activity, where their perception of time was 1 hour. Numerous experiments showed an accuracy of within 5–10 per cent of the correct timing of the sound.

These experiments by Erickson and Cooper appear to offer us a tantalising glimpse into the true power and speed of the subconscious. It is easy to see why Erickson and Cooper thought this technique could be used for other useful activities such as problem solving. Imagine if you are asked to solve a problem, you could just pop into self-hypnosis, spend an hour or two thinking about it, and then return to a conscious state 10 seconds later to report the answer.

Unfortunately, Erickson found that the activities suffered the same limitations as we now understand of the subconscious. Practising previously learnt activities, albeit at immense speed, was achievable. However, new 'creative' thought, and problem solving was not successful. It would appear that, although week and feeble, the conscious, logical brain really is required. We may have to put up with real time. However, it would appear to offer us interesting methods of practice.

For our purposes, these experiments give us an indication of the immense speed and power of the subconscious mind. It also leads me to a statement that you may well find great difficulty in accepting. Although, by deciding to purchase this book, and getting this far, I have already placed you in a small elite of intelligent, open-minded individuals who will evaluate new ideas on their merit. So to the statement:

> *All decisions we take are taken by the subconscious. If necessary, the conscious mind invents a 'logical' justification for the decision. In effect, the conscious brain is in a constant state of delusional belief that it is in control.*

You may want to take a few moments to think about this one. If it is true, then it offers us a route to manipulating people via their subconscious. A social engineer ultimately wants to control people to a degree that allows them to accomplish an attack. If the subconscious really is in control then attacks utilizing the subconscious will be more effective.

The Power of Commands

Examples:

The first example is a simple one of someone doing an action (subconsciously) they instantly regret (consciously).

If you have young children you will have probably experienced this first hand. If you don't have any then I recommend you borrow one to experiment with.

Imagine you are sitting comfortably and your young child slowly enters the room. They are moving very slowly and carefully as they are carrying a glass of milk, rather too full for your liking. They haven't seen you there, so their first idea of your presence is when you say, 'Don't drop that!'

Now that does seem a sensible thing to say. However, they instantly drop the milk on your new living room carpet and then look horrified. So what happened? Well, firstly it was your fault. Yes, you told them to do it.

You have to understand that logic is the preserve of the conscious brain. Upon hearing your command (it will be interpreted as a command if given by a dominant adult), the subconscious can't understand 'don't', and so just hears (and obeys) 'drop that!'. It does work better with parents giving the command as you will have effectively conditioned the child since an early age to follow your instructions. It can still work with other people's children so it is still worth borrowing one to experiment on. Clearly it doesn't work as well with teenagers who are busy conditioning themselves to avoid anything their parents ask of them.

Anyway, back to the child standing above the dropped glass. Their subconscious reacted to your command, taking the decision to let go. This happens very quickly (within the first second). The conscious brain also heard the words, and has now (much more slowly) applied the following logic:

- 'don't' = do the opposite of the words that follow;

- 'drop that' = drop something, probably this glass;

- 'don't drop that' = I must keep hold of this glass. Oops. Too late.

By the time the conscious brain has worked all that out, the glass has already hit the floor. In such circumstances you probably blamed the child. The child will in all probability be mortified and get quite upset, unable to justify their action (at a conscious/logical level).

A good second example of the power of the subconscious, and its control over our decisions, is the area of smoking. The world has large numbers of people who consciously would love to 'give up'. However, the subconscious mind doesn't agree. Now, I don't really want to write a book on this subject as there are already plenty. However, there are a couple of observations I would like to make and I certainly recommend the hypnosis route for anyone wishing to treat the lungs to fresh air.

The term 'giving up' is a terrible one. All our subconscious associations with that term are negative. Remember parents saying 'don't give up ...'. Instead of giving up, why not 'adopt an invigorating lifestyle' and 'breathe only the freshest air'.

Secondly, the heart of the problem is that the subconscious is immune to the conscious logic that smoking can lead to long-term health problems. Therefore, the subconscious simply needs some immediate, and current, negative associations with smoking that are stronger than its existing positive associations. It will then decide to give up.

It is interesting to listen to a smoker's innovative conscious reasoning as to why they haven't stopped smoking when they are 'trying'. By the way, 'trying' to do something is not an empowering description. People that 'try' usually don't actually complete an activity. Rather than 'trying', why not 'just do it'.

Now if you are particularly analytical (please see the previous chapter if you need to understand your personality profile), then you may want some more scientific explanation of the assertion that the subconscious is so critical to decision making.

Ideally we could open someone's brain and break the connection between the conscious logical brain and the subconscious emotional side of the person. Now, without needing to ask for volunteers, there happens to be some interesting case studies on some unfortunate individuals that give us a reasonable alternative source of data. I refer here to the cases described so excellently by Antonio Damasio in his book *Descartes' Error*.

THE CASE OF PHINEAS P. GAGE

The first case is quite well known and concerns an individual named Phineas P. Gage. In 1848, Phineas was a 25-year-old railway foreman, helping to construct a new line across Vermont, USA. Phineas had considerable expertise in the use of explosives and was busy blasting his way through rock.

The technique being used by Phineas involved drilling a hole, inserting explosives, and then packing this down with sand, using a long iron rod. Unfortunately, a simple slip up saw Phineas hammer the rod down directly on to the explosive with devastating consequences. The rod shot into Phineas' face, entering his cheek and exiting through the top of his head, near the forehead. The explosion was such that the rod then travelled a further hundred feet. For those people who want more precise details of the trajectory, you can see the skull (along with the iron rod) at the Warren Medical Museum.

As you may well have guessed, the interesting thing about Phineas is that he survived. Other than a nasty infection in the wound that developed over the next few days, he had surprisingly little in the way of direct effects from the injury. He didn't even lose consciousness. A local newspaper, that clearly hadn't developed the modern art of headline writing, summed it up in the title 'Passage of an iron rod through the head'. His 'recovery' was rapid and he was declared cured in less than 2 months. However, all was not as it seemed.

In 'normal' terms, Phineas' brain wasn't damaged. His memory was intact, both short term and long term. Neither were his language skills affected. All his senses were functioning as normal. However, his life began to fall apart! To quote his doctor, as documented by Damasio, he was, 'Fitful, irreverent, indulging at times in the grossest profanity which was not previously his custom, manifesting but little deference for his fellows, impatient of restraint or advice when it conflicts with his desires, at time pertinaciously obstinate, yet capricious and vacillating, devising many plans of future operation, which are no sooner arranged than they are abandoned.' (He had a doctor with a fantastic vocabulary.)

Given that this case happened more than 150 years ago, it is difficult to make detailed observations or conclusions. However, if you take the time to read Damasio's account you could summarize Phineas' problem as the loss of decision-making capability. What fascinates me about this case is that his range of conscious, logical faculties remained, yet he still couldn't make 'sensible' decisions.

Is this the evidence that the subconscious is so critical in decision making? Is what Phineas lost the capacity to receive messages from his subconscious?

Damasio takes a more mainstream academic approach, if judged radical by some, of exploring the role of emotions in decision making. I am taking a more NLP-centric view of the world in my conclusions.

ELLIOT'S CASE HISTORY

A more modern case, and one of Damasio's own patients, therefore giving us a much more detailed case history, is that of Elliot. In Elliot's case the damage to the front of the brain came from a tumour. Although benign, the tumour was large enough to damage the surrounding brain tissue as a result of the pressure it exerted. Elliot survived surgery to remove the tumour, only to then develop symptoms very similar to those of Phineas.

However, given the recent timeframe, Damasio was able to subject Elliot to a wide range of well-respected psychological assessments. As with Phineas, his full range of logical, conscious, faculties were intact. In fact Damasio was 'impressed by Elliot's intellectual soundness'. Across a wide range of assessments, Elliot performed to a level of 'superior intellect'. What fascinated Damasio was that someone with such a problem could not be shown to be deficient in any of the standard psychological and neuropsychological tests.

Elliot even performed well in tests as interesting as the 'how many giraffes are there in New York City?' assessment. This is an involved question, as it requires a wide range of intellectual (logical) techniques to solve. Firstly, you need general memory to know that giraffes don't live in New York and then detailed memory to identify that there may in fact be some in zoos, and so on. You then need to estimate the number of such locations and the probable number of beasts at each location. Therefore, your final answer is built from many components. This estimation exercise demonstrates a wide range of facilities. Not only that, according to the experts, it works equally well with elephants. Elliot could cope with both species.

Despite 'all' his mental abilities remaining intact, as with Phineas, Elliot's life began to disintegrate, characterized by loss of all sensible decision-making capability. When given a task at work, Elliot would understand the task, and begin, only to get bogged down in the minute analysis of some minor facet and unnecessary detail, at the expense of the whole task. People who knew about his background could not understand such 'flawed business and financial decisions'. The 'machinery for his decision making was so flawed that he could no longer be an effective social being'.

When relieved of his employment, Elliot spent his time formulating business plans, however, he never took any decisions with regards to actual implementation.

I would not go so far as to claim Damasio's work is fully supportive of the above conscious/subconscious decision-making claim. And I would recommend you read his excellent book and draw your own conclusions.

I conclude that Elliot had lost his subconscious ability to make decisions, using my frames of reference. In effect, Phineas and Elliot could no longer receive those essential decision messages from the subconscious. Interestingly, as I describe the decisions being made outside the realm of our conscious will, Damasio characterized Elliot's problem by saying his 'free will had been compromised'.

So, is it true that the subconscious makes all our decisions? Asking you to make a decision as to whether it is your conscious or subconscious that makes your decisions could be tricky. Perhaps one day I will try and construct a watertight piece of verbal logic to prove the concept. However, even with examples that serve to prove the point, how many people find it hard to accept that they live in a state of constant delusion?

We could just take the pragmatic view of 'truth'. Does it help us to move our understanding forward? I suggest that, in the context of explaining the ways that people can be persuaded, and manipulated, it is a useful theory. It certainly will help us as we move into new areas of psychology to help us develop frameworks to understand, test and develop countermeasures related to social engineering. One key conclusion is that our efforts should not be wholly focused on awareness and training activities that by their nature are targeted at the conscious brain.

One technique that does target the subconscious directly is that of hypnosis. There is a now a growing recognition that the subconscious can be influenced in more subtle ways, and these are being exploited to persuade, and sometimes exploit.

Our primary goal in this section of the book is to explore areas of psychology that you may not be familiar with. This gives us a context of understanding to build models for social engineering attack and methods of protection in the final section of the book. It is worth remembering that an attacker may be also studying these concepts and using them to develop more sophisticated methods to breach information security. One example is the use of hypnotic language.

Hypnotic Language

> *'By now, you can see how this book is clearly right for you. Tell me, do you have any remaining concerns about the benefits it will give you?'*

The above is an example of typical language from a salesperson. They may have been specifically trained in this form of words, picked them up from someone else, or just stumbled across them through trial and error. Or, they may be very clever. On the surface, the two sentences are very simple. Our logical (conscious) mind can understand the words and should be replying to the question in the second sentence.

However, something else is going on here. Your subconscious mind is receiving another set of messages. These messages are 'hidden' in the text. The effect they have will largely depend upon the level of rapport you have, and your current level of hypnosis.

Let's unpick the words and find the hidden meaning, assuming that the hidden messages are deliberate:

The first sentence contains *'you can see'* and indicates that the speaker is targeting the visual side of the target. The speaker may have identified the listener's dominant communication method or they may just be going with the majority and guessing it will work.

Next, *'this is clearly right for you'* is an instruction. It uses the politician's favourite vague word *'clearly'*. This cleverly gives the listener the chance to insert their own 'picture' of why it is right for them.

The next sentence is a question, at least consciously and grammatically it is. However, the inclusion of *'tell me'* at the beginning, turns it more into an instruction to answer. The conscious brain ignores the opening words and just listens to the question. The subconscious gets an instruction to answer the question. This is important here as the salesperson is trying to uncover any objection to the sale.

However, perhaps the most potentially 'underhand' inclusion are the very first two words. Another throwaway opening, *'by now'*. The conscious brain ignores these as superfluous to the sentence. The subconscious effect of these words? Perhaps they should have been correctly spelt *'buy now'*. Clearly this has to be a salesperson's opening.

CHALLENGE

Without turning to the next page, reread the introduction to this book and find as many hidden commands as you can. Here are some:

- 'you can think about human security'

- 'you will see'

- 'you will learn from this book'

- 'find the contents accessible'

- 'learn some of the techniques for yourself'

- 'feel free to proceed'

- 'you can get in touch'

These are examples of where a subconscious input can be hidden from the conscious brain (assuming normal reading or listening and not detailed analysis). This direct subconscious manipulation is the key to many persuasion techniques, and is now increasingly been seen in the armoury of a social engineering attacker.

Better Model of the Mind

As we explore these techniques we can develop the model of the mind, as shown in Figure 7.3.

We now have inputs being fed into the conscious mind, and also directly into the subconscious, either when we are operating 'on automatic pilot' or as hidden 'subliminal' communication. The 'strength' of the conscious brain at that point in time will dictate the extent to which communication can directly influence the subconscious. The conscious brain can either compliment or counter the subconscious communication. We will be coming back to the issue of 'strength' of the conscious brain to intercept subconscious commands when we explore the development of social engineering protection in the next section of the book.

The actions, or outputs, are directly from the subconscious, with the conscious brain left as the deluded observer.

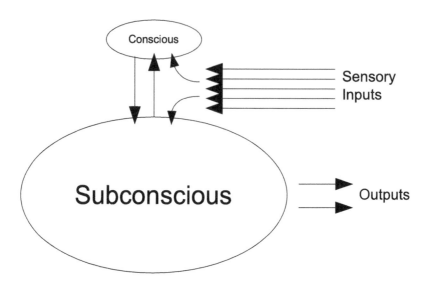

Figure 7.3   Advanced model of the mind

Enhanced Personality Profiling

These greater distinctions between the conscious and subconscious can allow us to develop our Personality Profiling Model (see Figure 7.4) and view the personality traits from a different perspective. You will find this useful as you seek to understand the particular vulnerabilities within certain target groups in your organization.

These observations may give you concern as to the vulnerability of security guards and call centre operators. Your concern is justified. However, you shouldn't interpret the above to mean that management and researchers are immune to attack. Far from it. The above should be taken in context of the fact that everyone is vulnerable, just to differing degrees and requiring different modes of attack and associated protection.

LET'S GO 'PHISHING'

We are now seeing a number of social engineering techniques being adopted by attackers in 'phishing' attacks. It is a measure of the vulnerability of the financial institutions' systems that many attacks have been so successful. This is without the attacker showing much in the way of advanced social engineering awareness or skills. However, remember that even a 0.1 per cent 'success' rate can be very rewarding.

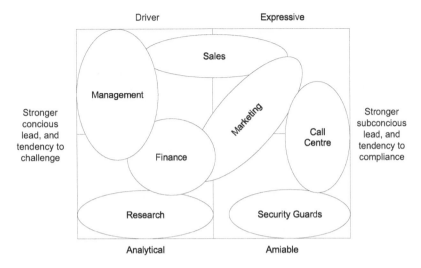

Figure 7.4 Personality profiles tendency to comply or challenge

Banks, and other online financial transaction accounts, are targeted because they are vulnerable. The commercial success of online access, rather than the cost of running a branch network, makes the risk of compromise acceptable to the bank. Having been involved in a number of risk assessments for financial institutions, the cost of these frauds often runs into millions of pounds. However, the cost of mitigation is still greater than the losses.

The fundamentals of current online banking systems do not put security first. From a technical viewpoint, allowing access into banking systems from uncontrolled home PCs is asking for trouble. Many home PCs are now routinely hacked to steal login details as you access your accounts. Phishing is the non-technical route to gaining your details. Setting up a fake online banking site is relatively easy and can be accomplished in, say, 1 hour, having hacked an insecure computer somewhere in the world. This could be another home PC on a broadband connection or a vulnerable web server.

The attacker then constructs an email which appears to be a communication from your bank, tricking you into clicking on a link and logging into a site you believe is your online account. Your login details are then collected and used to transfer funds.

This attack relies on the ignorance of the user, and in some cases uses flaws in the banks' websites to hide further the fact that you are sending your details elsewhere.

It is worth pointing out that a reasonably well tried and tested solution to this problem is in use in many countries. A smart card, or token, is used in conjunction with the login credentials to ensure that only you can access your account. This 'two-factor' authentication, whilst not 100 per cent secure, goes a long way to prevent the routine phishing attacks. We see:

- The banks are well aware of the solutions, so why don't they act?

- The cost of the solution is greatly in excess of their current losses.

- They are concerned about customers questioning the security of online banking and losing confidence in their systems.

The fraudsters keep exploiting the vulnerabilities and continue to make handsome returns. The lack of action by the major banks is evidenced by the fact that attacks have tended to concentrate on a relatively small number of target institutions. Given that the banks are not responding effectively, the attackers have not had to move on to smaller, and less profitable, targets.

One countermeasure the banks have deployed is to try and 'educate' their users, raising their security awareness, usually delivered through their website. Messages may be along the lines of, 'We will never send you an email asking you to login into your account,' accompanied by 'useful' advice about home PC security.

This strategy, whilst good in its intentions, is flawed. It positions the bank, in the minds of its users, as the source of security advice. Therefore, when a user receives a new communication from the bank, they have been pre-programmed to follow the instructions if it relates to security. Remember, when it comes to IT, the majority of the population feel ignorant. They know that they must follow the instructions of the experts.

So, let us explore some specific psychological tricks that could be used in a phishing attack by examining a sample email shown in Figure 7.5.

Now, this just needs to be combined with some effective design and a realistic fake site to collect the compromised security details. Of course, a really elegant attack would use existing security-related communication mechanisms of the bank to give the reader a link from previous messages, using the institution's own security countermeasures to aid an attack.

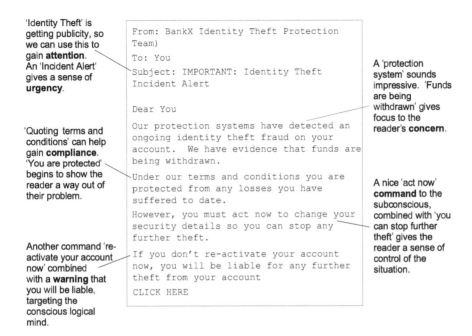

'Identity Theft' is getting publicity, so we can use this to gain **attention**. An 'Incident Alert' gives a sense of **urgency**.

'Quoting terms and conditions' can help gain **compliance**. 'You are protected' begins to show the reader a way out of their problem.

Another command 're-activate your account now' combined with a **warning** that you will be liable, targeting the conscious logical mind.

A 'protection system' sounds impressive. 'Funds are being withdrawn' gives focus to the reader's **concern**.

A nice 'act now' **command** to the subconscious, combined with 'you can stop further theft' gives the reader a sense of control of the situation.

```
From: BankX Identity Theft Protection
Team)
To: You
Subject: IMPORTANT: Identity Theft
Incident Alert

Dear You
Our protection systems have detected an
ongoing identity theft fraud on your
account.  We have evidence that funds are
being withdrawn.
Under our terms and conditions you are
protected from any losses you have
suffered to date.
However, you must act now to change your
security details so you can stop any
further theft.
If you don't re-activate your account
now, you will be liable for any further
theft from your account
CLICK HERE
```

Figure 7.5   Psychological analysis of a phishing attack

Some recent, and particularly cheeky, examples are giving security advice in the phishing email itself. This provides further reassurance for the user that this message must be coming from their banks.

The banks are well aware that the use of proper two-factor authentication (such as the use of hardware tokens with ever changing numbers) is the best current protection against phishing. However, their losses are not yet to the level where the investment in technology makes economic sense. Although we are seeing some 'pilot' schemes, it will probably take regulatory changes to force all the banks into migrating to more secure methods for online banking and related activities.

Parent, Adult, Child

8

Imagine a social engineering attacker is about to socially engineer someone. They are watching the target carefully and are close enough to hear them interacting with others. They now have a decision to make. What role are they going to adopt?

As an attacker's social engineering skills and experience develop, they may develop to a level where they can switch roles in an instant, depending upon the situation. This is what I find so fascinating in this field of information security. When planning for social engineering testing, I always remember to remain very flexible and change tactics if necessary.

For example, in a recent testing, I was entering a reception to trick my way past security guards and through a swipe entry system. I initially tried to persuade them (in a subtle way) that I was an employee. They challenged me by asking to see my ID. I then switched roles to a visitor and produced my (fake) visitor badge. This led to a successful bypass of their systems. This ability to switch roles, depending upon the reading of the target, can be extremely useful.

Roles for the Social Engineer

During my early presentations on social engineering, I outlined some useful roles for the social engineer.

NEW TECHNICIAN

Working well for on-site attacks, this role has two main advantages, and I use it regularly (luckily my surprisingly youthful looks still allows me to do this convincingly).

Firstly, it gives you a good excuse for doing technical things, from inspecting PCs (good for planting key loggers) to carrying out surveys that require you to record logins and passwords. Most staff just accept most things that a 'technical' person tells them; if it doesn't make sense then this just reinforces their belief that they don't understand IT.

Secondly, as a new employee you have the perfect reason why people don't recognize you. Being new also helps get a little sympathy and understanding that you don't quite know how things work. This is important for a social engineer, as no matter how much preparation you put in there will always be aspects of the organization that you haven't got quite spot on. Being new helps to explain any mistakes in 'how things are done around here'.

SECURITY CONSULTANT

On the basis that a role close to your 'real life' role is easier to carry off convincingly, I do find this an easy one.

The main advantage of this role is that you are there to ask plenty of questions about information security. Taking the role of an auditor is very similar, except that people are very used to giving auditors copies of every document they ask to see. I have used this role and been given copies of things that I didn't even ask for!

In fact, I find this role is so easy and productive that I rarely use it. I personally find the need to be a little more creative than just being myself and I find my clients expect the same. Also, I always suspect clients may find it unrealistic, as how many attackers would be experienced consultants and know exactly how they behave? Also, I do like a challenge, and using new and different roles can give interesting results that I can learn from and the client gets to uncover new insights into their security.

MANAGER

A good solid role for most social engineering situations. In general, people expect to receive instructions from managers. Employees also, on occasion, expect to be pressured into taking immediate action by managers. In addition, new managers sometimes like to make an impact, explaining the urgency of your requests. As a new (explains why people don't recognize you) manager you also may be making strange requests due to your inexperience in the organization.

These are all useful to the social engineer, and a manager role is tried and tested. I find that to be convincing you need to put the manager in a context, and have gathered some organizational knowledge.

One trick I find useful is to gain as much information as you can about a manager in the organization, and then to adopt their role completely with one exception – a different name. Almost a method acting role, getting 'into the skin' of the adopted role and their position within the organization. There is a reason that most managers behave the way they do, and it is because it gets them results in a given organization; using this helps you to adopt a realistic role within the same environment.

POTENTIAL CUSTOMER

As a general rule, organizations fall over backwards to satisfy customers – remember the customer is king! A social engineer will use this to aid their attack. If you gather information about existing customers, then you can adopt a role from that organization to help the attack. This can be useful remotely or face-to-face.

One trick I particularly like is to adopt the role of a new person in a buying position who wants to come and inspect the operation at their key supplier. Usually people will be making every effort to satisfy every request.

An interesting twist to this attack is to visit the supplier of your target organization, pretending to be from your target. As part of the visit you can request copies of various pieces of information that the supplier holds about the target. If the service is sufficiently important you can obtain your ultimate goal without ever having to directly attack the target. Another great reason why we should all be checking the security levels in our key suppliers and monitoring the information they hold that we value and which would be a useful target to someone else.

Another advantage of using the customer role is that you often get quite generously looked after by the target organization, especially if you target the sales staff. However, I am careful about using this in social engineering testing, as taking expensive sales people off their role of bringing in sales for too long can be costly.

BUSINESS PARTNER

Other types of business partners can be useful roles, building on existing relationships, especially where these relationships involve the sharing of information on a regular basis. In similar ways to the methods above that exploit the customer relationship, other business partnerships can be equally useful.

CO-WORKER DEVELOPING RAPPORT

A general approach of pretending to be a co-worker making friends can always be useful. I find this approach helpful for those small on-site encounters during an attack, or for a variety of telephone approaches during initial information gathering stages of an attack.

AUTHORITY FIGURE

The use of authority carries some risks, especially as it can annoy the target and may lead to them talking to other people about the incident. However, it can be useful in the situation where you need quick action.

Also, in situations where you just don't know how to react then 'losing it' can be quite realistic. It also tends to get a basic subconscious response from the target, often completely different from their previous behaviour. Some people, when faced with an authority figure throwing their weight around, will just take the line of least resistance and capitulate.

Personally, I don't like this approach as it doesn't help develop an effective relationship with the target. However, in some situations it gets quick results and therefore should be in the armoury of any self-respecting social engineer.

REMOTE WORKER IN AN EMERGENCY

This is especially useful where you can adopt the role of a salesperson, especially the night before a key sales presentation when you need remote access to the valuable files that will make all the difference between making the multi-million sale or not.

If you find remote access requires a hardware token two-factor authentication, then a call to the helpdesk with the above scenario (have lost your token) can often uncover alternative access methods for use in such emergencies.

FINDING ROLES THAT WORK

The roles above are a good starting point and each have their advantages when the situation is right. I encourage my fellow social engineering testers to be creative and flexible, finding roles that have the right impact with the client, yet that can also work for them.

If you are lucky enough to find yourself leading a team of social engineering testers, then understanding the personalities of the testers can be just as important as finding information about the target.

In one recent test, I had the challenge of using an engineer who was conducting his first test. I needed his technical skills for the activities we were to carry out once we were on-site. At the point we were breaking in, I decided that he just didn't have a convincing persona for the roles we were adopting so I gave him a simple instruction. He was to ring someone on his mobile phone as we entered, therefore distracting him whilst leaving me to do the talking. This also gave him something to distract his conscious brain with and stop him looking so worried.

Applying Transactional Analysis

In this chapter, I want to explore some of these social engineering roles and use a well-established psychology framework to help you understand some of the attack interactions.

Each of the above roles has its merits, however, you should base your decision on two main points:

1. matching the role to the target;

2. adopting a role you can play convincingly.

The second point does remind me of a conversation I had with a client who had defined a very narrow set of social engineering tests for us to carry out. His analysis included the role to be adopted, what was to be said and even the exact timing of the attacks. Our first observation was that the proposed testing was rather too narrow. After all, clients use our social engineering services to uncover those vulnerabilities they are not aware of, not to test one simple scenario.

Another observation I made was that perhaps adopting the role of a local electricity engineer, as suggested, may not be the most convincing role or even be achievable. For example, his budget did not stretch to the preparation of an appropriate vehicle, clothing, and so on. But more importantly, was this a role we could convincingly use? As it happens, my first degree was in electrical and electronic engineering so perhaps I could adopt the role well enough to gain entry. However, his 'story' to be used to gain access (ultimately to his server room) didn't sound realistic to us.

It was commendable that he had recognized social engineering as a real threat and wanted to test his countermeasures. After further consultation and discussion we formulated a new plan with enough flexibility to give a true test and also target his priority areas.

As a starting point, you should put yourself in the mind of the social engineer and start to think of the roles you would find most comfortable. Remember, this really is acting, and the closer to reality you are, the easier you will find it and, more importantly, the more believable you will be.

However, there are some techniques you can use to achieve results as a social engineering tester. For example, many roles allow you to become agitated as part of the scenario. Think of a salesperson trying to get remote access to the office network late at night to finish a critical (and very lucrative) customer proposal. In this scenario, you can always lose your cool and still be very convincing.

If you remember, you must also match the role to the target. So assuming you are now developing a range of roles to adopt, which one do you choose?

If you are to be really effective, you must get inside the target's head. Will they respond to pressure? Tenderness? Jokes? So let's enter the realm of psychoanalysis. If this is new to you, then you need to recognize that you do the following types of analysis every day. In fact, every time you interact with a fellow human being. As you learn some simple frameworks you will be able to think more clearly and use these techniques to your advantage.

So, let's start to explore Transactional Analysis (TA). This framework is very useful for social engineering due to its focus on interaction. As we have already explored, body language analysis is useful for 'reading' someone. However, most people never get beyond the 'let's copy what you do to develop rapport' stage. This book is not about social rapport building, we want to engineer the target into our desired action. We need to lead not follow.

TA helps us understand the thoughts and feelings of an individual and predict (and control!) how they may react to a given action on your part. Just for a moment, think back to your school days. Think of a few teachers that REALLY scared you. They probably made an impact before you reached, say 13 (after this age the 'bully' techniques used to control children begin to fail). Did you ever meet one of these teachers as an adult? Chances are you had all the same feelings of dread – with no 'logical' reason for such feelings. You probably even felt a little 'childish' afterwards for still reacting in such a way. Your 'adult' logic was probably telling you not to be so silly! Similar to the ongoing tension you may feel to your parents, as they still act the 'parent' even though you are no longer a child.

This way of characterizing our behaviour, and associated feelings, using the interaction between parents, children and between adults is fundamental to the TA framework.

TA is usually used as a therapy tool. It has value in helping people to be more autonomous, living in the present instead of being constrained by past experiences. An extension of TA is the concept of people living through 'scripts' where their behaviour is repetitive and predictable.

Within TA treatment, the therapist is often helping the patient to develop more of an awareness of the 'here and now'.

In the context of social engineering, I am interested in using the TA framework to understand the behaviours of individuals. This can be particularly useful in predicting how people may react to particular circumstances.

TA describes our personalities as falling into one of three 'ego states' – parent, adult or child (see Figure 8.1).

PARENT

The 'parent' ego state is where you feel, think, act, talk and respond as your parents did when your were little (or parent figures in your life – remember teachers are 'loco-parentis').

This learned behaviour tends to be mirroring parental behaviour, yet may be exhibited in other situations, such as conflict.

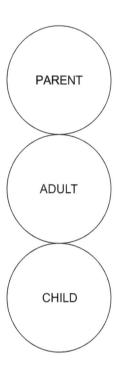

Figure 8.1   Transactional analysis ego states

ADULT

When you view the world objectively, calculate chance based on experience and logic, you are firmly in your 'adult' state.

This state is more a calculated reaction to the current environment. You could say this is a more conscious state of mind.

CHILD

When your feelings and responses are more as they were when you were a child (remember someone making you feel 'so small'?), then you are in your 'child' ego state.

ADDING MORE LAYERS

These finer distinctions can help you understand human interactions in more depth. Remember our aim here is to understand the transaction so we can control its direction and outcome. For example, splitting the PARENT into two:

1.   The *nurturing parent* – often described as the mother figure;

2.   The *controlling parent* – often described as the father figure.

This obviously assumes the mother is the nurturing type and the father is the controlling type. There are other distinctions, such as splitting the child into two further states:

1.   The *free child* – the fun side of a child, uninhibited and free;

2.   The *adaptive child* – tries to please the adults around it.

You may want to explore these further if you find this framework useful in understanding social engineering interactions.

The descriptions are obviously generalizations, however, I am sure you are starting to get the picture. Let's put this in context of social engineering. An initial look at our social engineering roles above, could give us some typical TA ego states:

Role	Typical TA ego state
New technician	*adaptive child* – assuming being new to the role makes you feel quite insecure
Security consultant	*adult* – although holding some authority, the consultant should not assume control, rather remaining in an analytical state
Manager	*parent* (either *nuturing* or *controlling*) or *adult* – depending upon the management 'style' adopted
Potential customer	*adult* – may well be analysing the benefits of the buying option
Business partner	*adult* – assuming the relationship is at a professional level
Co-worker developing rapport	*free child* – relaxing and having fun
Authority figure	*parent* – controlling of course
Remote worker in an emergency	*adaptive child* – helpless and needing support or *controlling parent* – demanding action

I have called these typical ego states, as the specific state adopted is usually dependent upon the specific interactions and, more crucially in the context of social engineering, the ego state adopted by the other person in the interaction. However, it gives you some examples to think about. I suggest you observe people and try to place them into an ego state; remembering that the state will change dependent upon the particular interaction they may be in at the time.

Someone taking on the role of an authority figure, say a manager, will often adopt the *controlling parent* persona, giving instructions in an assertive way that gets results. By adopting the role of a *parent*, treating the target as a *child*, the natural response from the target can be directed to that of the *child*. This does depend upon the usual behaviour of the target and their perceived place in the hierarchy of the work environment. An attacker would get more success trying this with a junior secretary than with a senior executive.

If this *parent* role is being adopted by a social engineer, they will be working on the assumption that they will get results. The reaction you want is the *child* from the target. This is a natural reaction, as most of us have many influential years of this transaction, an example being told what to do by a teacher.

If the target (*child*) believes the person making the demands is who they say they are, then it is likely they will respond by doing as they are told.

TA can be expressed in diagrams to show transactions such as the one shown in Figure 8.2.

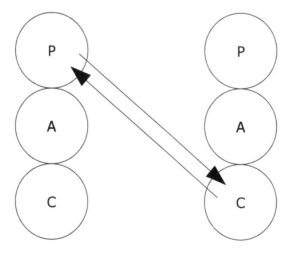

Figure 8.2   Transactional analysis transaction diagram

The left-hand side shows the three ego states of the attacker, with the right-hand side showing the equivalent states of the target.

It is important to remember that the *child* response may be in some ways directed, with the *parent* nature of the social engineering attacker forcing the target to feel uncomfortable. If people are forced out of their comfort zone, then a reaction can be to revert to *child*-like behaviour. However, given the sometimes unpredictable nature of human psychology, the attacker may get the opposite reaction. Some people may react aggressively, exhibiting more *parental* behaviour themselves.

Alternatively, imagine that the target gets suspicious. Perhaps they have had some social engineering training and think, 'Do I know who this person is?' Their logic (*adult*) begins to assess the situation and formulates a response. Perhaps they ask a probing question: 'I am very sorry to stop you there, perhaps you could just explain who you are so I can help you?'

Rather than the intended, compliant *child* response, the attacker receives an *adult* reply

This has been phrased as to still be quite helpful and not too offensive. This is a good idea for staff training exercises as you don't want all requests for help (even if delivered forcefully) to be met with aggression. This would be a *parent* to *parent* reply. It is useful to remember that when stressed, many people find it easier to fall into the *critical parent* or *adaptive child* states.

In the case of the *adult* response shown above, not only is the response coming from the target's *adult*, yet is directed at the manager's *adult*. The question expects a reasonable response. You can further your TA expertise by referring to the above as a 'crossed transaction' (see Figure 8.3).

So how would the manager, or a social engineer adopting this role, react to this situation?

- They often become more forceful, with a more exaggerated *parent* state. This is trying to force the other person into submission, in effect rejecting the *adult* response and continuing to force them into the *child* state.

- They could themselves drop into the *adult* state, giving logical reasoning for their request.

- They could even make a joke of the situation, dropping into the *free child* state. This can have the advantage of also taking the target into a *child* state too, taking them away from the *adult*.

The general strategy is to break from the crossed transaction.

You can see from the above options that analysis can get complex and can change from one part of a conversation (transaction) to another. Two people can flip between all three states many times within one conversation. It would not be appropriate to fill the rest of the book with a multitude of diagrams, however I hope you see the possibilities to characterize certain responses to social engineering tactics. This can help us formulate appropriate training and other protection mechanisms.

You may observe that the worst state for the target to be in, from a social engineer's point of view, is the *adult* state. Here the target is more likely to recall training, question actions and consciously think before they respond or act. This state is characterized by balanced, calm reasoning.

As you notice more examples of different *parent, adult, child* transactions in the people around you, you will begin to observe the art of social engineering in everyday conversation.

A master social engineering strategy is based on *everything* the target is telling the attacker about their likely next move. Here the other 'mind reading' skills, previously discussed, are useful.

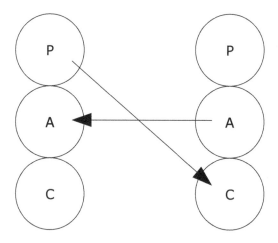

Figure 8.3   Crossed transaction

It is important to remember that no particular approach will be right in every situation. For example, in many instances when conducting social engineering testing, I will simply adopt an *adult* state. In this case my explanation for my actions and the requests I am making of the target are logical and stand up to logic questioning. The skill is in adopting a complementary state that enables the attacker to manipulate the target in the most efficient way.

ULTERIOR TRANSACTIONS

At this point, we are not satisfied with simply understanding transactions and knowing how each transaction fits into some clever model. To do justice to 'hacking the human' we really must move on to something a little more covert, using our knowledge of the subconscious.

In the following scenario we are going to communicate in a very *adult* manner. On the surface, a casual observer with some knowledge of TA may well think the interaction is purely *adult* to *adult*.

However, the underlying response is from the *parent* in the target. This ulterior transaction can be a powerful social engineering tool. The target can't quite understand 'why they did it'. Their *adult* logic only remembers the overt communication, however their own subconscious response (extensively *parent* led) confuses them.

The example previously used to demonstrate the power of the subconscious when a child drops the glass of milk is similar to this, with a subconscious reaction under a seemingly contradicting command.

In the following example, the commands used aim to gain the compliance required by the attacker.

The target is the executive assistant to the chief financial officer of a FTSE 100 company. The objective of the attack is to get the assistant to email a copy of a current (and highly confidential) tender document. The attack is conducted over the phone.

Previous research by the attacker has identified the key contacts at both the target company and their merchant bank advising them on the deal (all quite easy information to obtain):

'Hello, is that Janice?'

'Yes, how can I help you?'

'My name is Jerry Hitchings, Assistant to James Wilson-Harding, over here at BankA.'

'Oh yes, I don't think we've spoken before.'

'Yes, I'm quite new to ProjectBig, just been transferred 2 days ago to help out. Been some crazy hours here over the last few days, everyone is working flat out.'

'So you are right in the thick of it, I would guess, things are busy here too.'

'To be honest, it is getting a bit intense and sparks are flying, and now I've come in the office and all our main computer systems are down. I'm sure you've had things go wrong at just the worst time?'

'Oh yes, I'm sure IT create problems to have maximum impact on us.'

'Well I'm going to get the blame for this one if I can't prepare these documents in time. It isn't often that I feel scared, however this is one of them.'

'What is the problem?'

'I have to put together the latest update briefing and our response to those reports in the press yesterday. If I don't have this together in the next hour then I'm probably looking for another job.'

'How can I help?'

'Well luckily I have most of the material on my laptop, however I don't have the master tender document to cross-reference our response. I have promised this to James by 11:00 am, he is not in the mood for excuses even if our computers are down. He won't use a computer, so isn't very understanding.'

'I have the document here, can I help you?'

'Oh great, I was hoping that you can help me. I have got Internet access, so can receive things on my private email account.'

A few minutes later and a multi-billion pound confidential document is disclosed. Is the attack from a competitive bid or perhaps the press looking for more inside information? Alternatively, it could be someone looking to bet on the outcome with some share trading, where the inside information could be the key.

The above attack is a simplified example. As previously explained, trying to get information in a single call is quite high risk. A more effective strategy would be to build rapport and a relationship over time with a number of conversations. However, it serves our purpose of illustrating the concepts of applying TA to understanding the communication.

Although quite complex, the diagram of this interaction would look like the one shown in Figure 8.4.

The primary communication is *adult* to *adult*. However, within the communication are multiple commands and instructions, and this leads to the *parent* compliance with the instruction.

The above technique could well stretch the most skilled social engineering abilities. However, it gives you a goal as you bring together the range of techniques described in this book and reach a new level of personal mastery.

Of course our aim here is to understand the techniques and to begin to think about developing effective countermeasures to thwart an attack. That leads us neatly into the final section of this book.

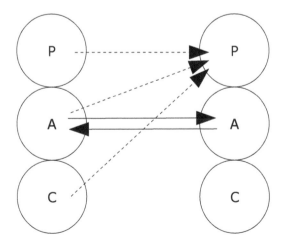

Figure 8.4   Using TA to map hidden communication

Countermeasures

Vulnerability Mapping

CHAPTER

9

It is commonplace now for companies to conduct technical vulnerability assessments for their IT systems. These assessments often combine automated scanning and audit tools with manual testing. It is now widely accepted that third-party testing is an essential part of IT security management. However, what are you trying to achieve with testing? Uncovering vulnerabilities that you were not previously aware of; something that people often forget when they repeat the same annual (external only) penetration testing. So your penetration testing goal, as part of your IT security provision, is to uncover and understand vulnerabilities.

The same principle of testing should be applied to the human element of your information security. In the final chapter of this book we shall be exploring social engineering testing in more detail, however, at this stage, I want to explore the wider understanding of vulnerabilities and to measure how protected your systems are to social engineering attack.

With an area of understanding at an early stage of development and comprehension, you will often find a lack of viable frameworks available to help you in your analysis; social engineering is no different.

In order to understand the vulnerabilities present in a given information system, I find it helpful to understand the Personnel Strength and Systemic Strength of the security within that system. I define these two variables of social engineering protection, as such:

Personnel Strength – the ability of the individuals within the information system to detect, and withstand, a social engineering attack.

Systemic Strength – the ability of the information system to withstand a social engineering attack without relying upon human intervention.

An example of Personnel Strength is where a helpdesk operator refuses to reset a remote access login without telephoning (internally) a line manager for confirmation.

An example of Systemic Strength is where someone tricked into sending a piece of information externally by email finds that the email is automatically blocked due to its information classification.

These variables give you an indication of how reliant you are on the people within your information security and whether you have compensating systems for their vulnerabilities.

There are situations where you will completely rely on your people to prevent a successful attack. For example, a system database administrator with access to external email may have the rights to attach the whole database data set (in a variety of formats) to an external email. Therefore, if successfully engineered by an attacker, they can be an immediate source of a major breach. In this situation, without additional technical restrictions, the Personnel Strength, as defined by their ability to detect and withstand a social engineering attack, is your only defence. In many organizations this situation, where people are only one email send away from releasing confidential information, is becoming the norm.

However, there are also scenarios where you can create a system that will not require the Personnel Strength to be a protection layer. For example, in a call centre you can restrict the operators' access to more than a single record at a time (assuming this still allows them to work) and not give them access to email or the ability to print. In very high-risk situations you could even restrict the use of pen and paper and photographic devices (including mobile phones). In effect, the only way information can be removed by an employee is to remember it – or leak it over the phone to a caller.

This substantially restricts the capability of the social engineer to target an employee in order to steal a whole database, the best they could get is the details of a single record. This can, in many situations, be more than adequate to save the organization from expensive breaches. Here the Systemic Strength gives you much less reliance on the individual.

By understanding the relative components of an information security management system, and the relevant risks present for the organization, you can direct management attention where it is most needed. The allocation of resources, whether the building of systemic improvements or additional staff training and awareness activities, can then be more efficient. In addition, it allows easy comparison of different systems within an organization and potentially between organizations (depending upon their willingness to share this sensitive information).

Therefore producing a measurement of the two components of system protection provides a good starting point to understanding your social engineering vulnerabilities. Especially when helping managers understand their vulnerabilities, it can be helpful to be able to produce graphical representations of risk.

You can map the systems on to a matrix, as shown in Figure 9.1.

Comparing System Strength

SYSTEM A

This information system has strong Systemic Strength that restricts the employees into following sound practices. In addition, you can see that Personnel Strength is relatively high; this is a measure of their understanding of social engineering threats and their ability to respond.

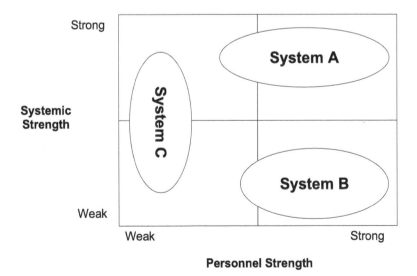

Figure 9.1   Social engineering system strength mapping

Systemic elements that fit into this category include strong authentication, segregation of duties and mechanisms forcing effective peer review of high-risk activities. The people employed are skilled and need to operate primarily in their conscious brain with plenty of variation in activities. This ensures a high level of awareness, combined with a tendency to question variations.

EXAMPLE – TECHNOLOGY COMPANY

In this example the company has, due to its technical competence, developed sophisticated sets of systemic controls to protect its critical information. In this case the most confidential information is the development programming code at the heart of its products. The storage of code is tightly controlled and regularly audited. This has removed the usual situation within development environments of all the developers having numerous copies of the code, including remote copies on removable media and personal computers.

The protection of this intellectual property is seen as key to the long-term value of the company and therefore its protection receives appropriate senior management support.

The spread of coverage in the mapping of System A represents the variations found within the staff involved in the system. Although the company has well-developed systemic protection, there is a variation in the vulnerability of their people. This is to be expected and we would be suspicious of any mapping that showed everyone measured with the highest levels of Personnel Strength.

SYSTEM B

In the case of our second example, System B, there are also strong elements of Personnel Strength. However, it has weak systems. This provides opportunities for attackers to target people, develop relationships and exploit weaknesses.

EXAMPLE – LAW FIRM

A legal practice can be a good example of this situation, with strong traditions of trust in people and the professional standards of employees. However, this can lead to complacency, both in assessing the vulnerability of fee earners to attack and also failing to understanding the range of support staff present within the system. It is easy to assume that the perceived professionalism of staff includes their ability to detect social engineering attacks – a dangerous assumption. There are now a wide range of support roles within most professional service organizations that do not have the same training, traditions and culture of confidentiality as you would expect within lawyers.

Two significant factors can lead to poor social engineering protection from systems within law firms:

1. The open nature of communication and the flow of information within the organization, where seniority can give you access to information.

2. A reluctance to spend money on systemic improvements. As partnership organizations are usually measured on profits per partner, there is a natural tendency not to invest in technical support systems, including information security.

Having said this, I am now encountering what I would call a 'new breed' of law firm. These organizations are recognizing the information security elements in their clients and responding with the development of similar protection mechanisms.

SYSTEM C

A common situation, especially within larger organizations, is to have a range of systems that map similarly to System C. Here the Personnel Strength is relatively weak, either through the types of people that can be afforded in the roles, or because the roles themselves lead to low levels of conscious activities due to boredom from repetition. Here the system strength varies across different aspects of the information system.

EXAMPLE – CALL CENTRE OPERATION

Because of the nature of call centres, with pressure to reduce staffing costs to a minimum (often through outsourcing to cheaper locations), the level of Personnel Strength is limited. This situation is compounded by high staff turnover, leading to a lack of investment in staff training and development as this is often seen as not necessarily delivering a return on investment.

In the example mapping above, you can see that although the Personnel Strength is low, there is a range of Systemic Strength. This is largely due to different call centre staff having different levels of access, depending upon the role they fulfil.

In this situation, targeting the areas where weak Personnel Strength combined with addressing the areas of weak Systemic Strength will have the greatest effect on raising the protection levels of the organization.

Mapping your Systems

In order to produce useful mappings of your systems, you can use the following methodology. I have used this approach with clients who were having difficulty identifying their social engineering vulnerabilities:

- Understand the threats to your information. This should be the starting point through your risk assessment. This helps you target your analysis into areas that will give you the greatest benefit.

- Assess the strength of your people. By measuring their ability to withstand attack you can start to build up the picture of your real security levels. This starts to take you away from the blind belief in a few technical countermeasures such as your firewall.

- Identify the systemic protection levels. The elements of your security that shield people and help you counter the ever present human vulnerabilities.

- Mapping your systems. This gives you a visual indication and comparison of different systems within your overall information security protection.

- Testing to confirm your assessments. At this stage your testing can be much more targeted and can help you make intelligent decisions.

- Implement improvements. By this stage you will have a clear action plan with a range of improvement strategies that give you a real return on any security investment. (Sounds so good it could be used in marketing!)

One slight word of warning: there are times when we are asked to do in-depth analysis of the type outlined above and we advise not to. Sometimes a level of information security protection, particularly with regard to social engineering, is so low that the required first steps are obvious. To use an analogy, I always advise that people at least start locking their front doors and close their windows (no pun intended) before investigating expensive alarm systems and CCTV.

If your social engineering vulnerabilities are obvious then we should help you fix them first before we embark on a more elaborate programme of analysis. Having said that, sometimes evidence and proof is required before decisions can be made, so you have to be flexible in your approach.

Section 1 of this book covered the understanding of social engineering threats in some detail, together with a variety of risk methodologies to help you assess their importance.

In the following chapters within this section we will be looking at important systemic protection countermeasures, developing appropriate staff training and the testing programme required. Therefore, in the rest of this chapter we shall be looking at techniques used to identify the strength of personnel within an organization. This is an area that I am evolving all the time. However, this will give you a glimpse into my current thinking and developing practice.

Although you can identify specific weaknesses and explore different attack vectors within a testing programme, you should not solely rely on this method to assess the overall strength of a given staff population within your organization. Testing is too limited in this respect, due to:

- Being quite labour intensive, and requiring a high level of expertise. Therefore it might only be conducted infrequently.

- Usually only covering a small sample of a given group of employees. These could also have been selected by the tests or dictated by the testing specification.

Therefore, we would not want to assume too many conclusions about the employees as a whole from a series of individual tests.

Also, as employees share information, it is highly unlikely you can conduct exactly the same social engineering test on a large population without the nature of the test becoming 'public' knowledge. Although you will see, when we explore testing in more depth, there are techniques you can use to minimize this risk.

Throughout Section 2 we explored a number of ways to look at the psychology of human vulnerabilities in relation to a social engineering attack. This included the concept of personality profiling. In this section I am going to show you some techniques for assessing this personality profile within a group of employees, enabling you to map their strength in relation to social engineering attack.

Personality Profiling Techniques

You may remember the enhanced personality profile mapping we previously explored.

The mappings in Figure 9.2 show some 'typical' groupings within an organization, based on my experience in analysis. You will remember that the left to right axis gives us an indication of the tendency to compliance in the context of a social engineering attack.

You must remember that any such activity as the above mapping is not 100 per cent for everyone. It does not mean that every individual would fit within the indicated boundaries; there are always notable exceptions to any mapping. Also, the 'tendency' to challenge or compliance is not a guarantee. A skilled social engineer will adopt the appropriate tactics and techniques for each target group. It does, however, give us a good indication to help our decision making. In common with other models of human thinking and behaviour we have discussed, if it is useful and helps us then we regard it as 'correct', if we find a more useful model then we switch to that.

My aim within the following illustration is to show you some development of techniques that can be used with larger numbers of employees to assess their personality profile in a cost-effective way. These techniques cannot give the level of accuracy that an attacker can achieve in assessing an individual as they learn about them in order to develop a 'working' relationship. However, mapping techniques can give you an overall indication of the tendency of

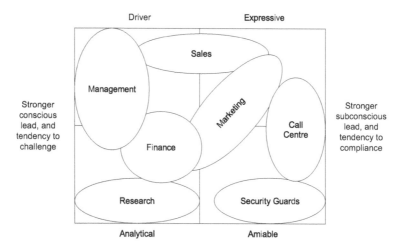

Figure 9.2   Personality profiles' tendency to comply or challenge

groups to be socially engineered and makes sense if you need to assess larger employee populations.

MAPPING QUESTIONS

I have found success with the use of questionnaires that allow me to uncover the various personality types within the different groups of people in an organization.

I do this by constructing a series of personality profiling questions. These questions are designed to uncover the specific traits that relate to the categories above. By mapping these we can then begin to understand the vulnerabilities that exist within a given population and identify the countermeasures that are needed to protect them.

Although I wouldn't want to give you a ready made consulting toolkit (I still have a consulting career to think about), here are a sample of questions to give you a good flavour of some of the activities.

I use a simple format, designed to illicit a quick response from the employee. I am looking for their unconscious first reaction or their quick initial response before they have time to think too deeply (and logically). I am also trying to get them not to give the answer they think their employer may want, rather a true answer for them.

They are reassured that no individual responses will be shared with their managers.

I often use the following example to show people how the system works:

As you can see, the employee simply places a cross on the line to indicate their preference towards one of the two statements. This example is to give them the idea of how the questions work. If actually used, this question would not tell me much about their personality.

An example of a genuine question is as follows:

Question 1: You have to solve a really difficult challenge at work, would you prefer to:

Act decisively, as inaction can be damaging		Get all the facts before you act, to avoid costly mistakes

This question gives two alternatives, and in each case indicates that not doing it this way would have negative consequences. An objective analysis would say that both statements can be correct in different circumstances. However, the belief system and personality profile of the individual will move them more in one direction.

In this question we are examining the range of response from Driver to Analytical:

Strong Driver		Strong Analytical

The response you get will usually not be at either of the two extremes of the scale, and this is fine. You also get responses in the middle and this is often an indication that the person is not either of the two personality types; often their response to other questions is more illuminating. As you will have seen above in the mappings, we expect a range of responses to mirror the range of personality types.

At times, when conducting this analysis with smaller groups, I also get the opportunity to observe the time taken to respond, sometimes to individual questions. In the above example, you often get a clear idea of the Drivers by their speed of response, and equally the strong Analyticals make themselves known by being last to finish (sometimes by a considerable time span, despite my instructions to go with their first impression for each answer).

Another example is:

Question 2: You have made a mistake that could affect a customer, would you prefer to:

| Do what is necessary to ensure you still look good | | Follow the established procedure, as this is the safest route |

Here we are examining a different axis:

| Strong Expressive | | Strong Amiable |

Here the response with the emphasis on looking good is likely to appeal to the Expressive side of someone's personality. You expect the sales people to be over on the left-hand side.

The 'safe' aspect of the alternative response is an indication that the person is likely to be an Amiable personality type.

Of course it is worth noting that, in the example above, how would you answer if you were neither Expressive nor Amiable? In this situation, you may find yourself saying, 'Well I don't agree with either of these statements.' If that is the case I would advise you to should place the cross in the middle to indicate no strong preference either way.

I have developed a number of ways to analyse the results. This can be quite complex, as people often do not record the extremes. In some cases I take a measure from each response of the extent to which people favour one extreme, and map this against each characteristic. On other occasions, I find simply reviewing the range of responses can give you insight into the personality profiles present.

I keep stressing to people that we are interested in their first reaction, 'going with their gut feeling'. Also, I ask people to answer each question relating to their work environment (assuming that I am trying to measure their personality profile in that context).

Asking a series of these questions allows us to map the combination of axis and produce the mappings seen in Figure 9.2 for each group of employees.

It is important to remember that in these personality profiling exercises we will always find exceptions. Although you can obtain useful information regarding the general trend within a group of employees, there will always be notable exceptions.

Also, I am very interested in the exceptions. If you have people who do not 'fit' then they may be candidates for unusual behaviour compared with their peer group. This could, in some circumstances, mean that could be the target (or even the source!) of an attack.

There are weaknesses in this type of profiling; a valid point for any tests conducted with simple questionnaires. There are also variations in personality; some people may not be typical of the people in similar positions, so you end up with individuals well outside the overall mapping for a given group.

From my own analysis, I have found numerous individuals who are notable for not being 'typical' for their profession. I am sure you can think of people who fit perfectly with the stereotypical profile for someone in their line of work, and also think of individuals who don't fit within this 'mould'.

The benefit of mapping personalities is that you can identify these variations and then allow for them when designing better social engineering protection mechanisms. With a tightly grouped set of personalities we can be more certain of their reaction to training and how they will deal with a given social engineering attack. When we see a wider spread of personalities we need to be more careful and plan for a wider range of reactions to specific attack vectors.

I have found these activities to be the basis of some quite advanced work with re-engineering systems to increase social engineering protection. They give a framework to understand human vulnerabilities and match that understanding of how protection countermeasures can help you manage the risk of social engineering. Whether this type of analysis is right for your organization will depend upon the nature of your activities, your current levels of protection and your decision-making processes.

Protection Systems

Probably the single biggest mistake that people make when thinking about social engineering protection, is to think only in terms of staff awareness. In our experience, given that awareness building tends to strengthen only the conscious processes, it is systemic improvements that are most effective in protecting your information.

A good example of a weak system, susceptible to social engineering attack, is that of a telephone helpline for a credit card provider. We came across an incident where an operator asked 17 questions of the caller to authenticate their identity before giving them access to their account. Yes, that is 16 wrong, or missing, answers and one correct answer. Now I make that 16 reasons not to give them access against one reason to grant access. Clearly, the bank's systems were giving the operator too many options and were too weighted on ease of use rather than security.

In another related example, one operator asked the customer if they could identify their last purchase. He asked for a clue (perhaps this should have been an alerting trigger!) and was told, 'It looks like golf clubs. Can you tell me how much they were?' The customer said he would have to check and call back. Later another call to a different operator had the same caller, when asked to identify their last purchase, saying, 'Oh yes, that will be the golf clubs.' So one operator is easily tricked into giving out information that another operator then accepts as valid authentication information. The bank's systems need to be improved to remove this vulnerability and give the operators less scope to give access to callers.

One good idea here is to limit operator questions, and, rather than refusing access, refer failing calls to a select team of more highly trained operators. This team can be given more flexibility to allow access in an emergency and trained in techniques to identify and track the fraudsters.

Building Systemic Improvements

In order to illustrate the value of systemic improvements, we will take four example social engineering attacks, analyse the way that people are targeted and develop systemic protection systems around the information to be protected.

Whilst focusing upon systemic improvements, I am not devaluing staff awareness and training (something that we will focus on in the next chapter). However, I want to stress that systemic improvements can be more effective in building protection layers that withstand more skilled attackers. It is worth pointing out that employees need training in the operation of new systems, however, this is more specific than just raising awareness and then relying on people spotting an attack.

ATTACK ONE – TELEPHONE ATTACK TO GAIN BANKING CREDENTIALS

This first attack is quite straightforward, targeted at an individual either at home or through their mobile telephone. Its intention is to obtain the necessary credentials to allow access to their telephone banking service.

It relies on two primary factors:

1. The target has to believe that the caller is from their bank. Given that most people will believe that the attacker is who they say they are, this can be a simple as, 'Hello, my name is XX, and I am calling from YY bank.' An improved strategy is to immediately follow this introduction with the reason for the call, such as, 'We have a problem with your current account that we need to resolve.' The worry factor of the second statement immediately takes the conscious processing away from questioning the first statement.

2. The target has to divulge enough necessary information for the attacker to use to gain access. This can be as simple as just asking the target to 'go through security, before we can resolve the problem'. A typical phrase could be, 'You will understand that we have to be very careful with security these days, so I will need to take you through security before we can resolve the problem.'

Of course the weakness that leads to this scenario is that the authentication is in the wrong direction. The caller (bank) knows who they are calling, or certainly knows the location they are calling in the case of a land line. The target does not know the identity of the caller; the attacker's strategy is to get the target to assume that the identity of the caller is genuine.

With banks and other financial institutions regularly making calls on this basis and using the same flawed authentication methods, this route of attack is relatively effective. Note: the current reassurance given by some banks that they will never ask for all your security details at the same time simply means the attacker may have to make two or three calls in order to sound convincing and be able to gather all the necessary information.

The caller needs the following information to launch the attack:

- the name of the person being called;

- the bank that they currently use;

- the authentication details currently in use by that bank.

Given that this type of attack is likely to be targeted at a number of individuals, one way of gathering this information would be to make some calls pretending to be conducting a survey of telephone banking (perhaps from a consumer group).

The carefully crafted survey would be designed only to get the name of the individual, whether they use telephone banking and which bank they use. The other questions would only be there to give the survey some realism. For example:

> *'Good evening, I hope I have caught you at a good time. I wonder if you can help me. If you would be so kind as to give me a few moments of your time, you can have a chance to win £500. We are doing a survey for the Financial Services Authority (FSA), I am sure you have heard of us. To take part you have to be a user of telephone banking, then all that happens is that you answer a few easy questions, taking about 2 minutes, and then you get the chance to win £500.'*

This speech is delivered in one go, without a break. This gives the caller chance to get the benefits over to you before you have a chance to say no. The 'easy' 2 minutes are outweighed by a chance to win the money.

A variation is for the attacker to say that the prize is an 'instant win' of £500, an extra little carrot to dangle. If you do win the caller can ask for your bank account details so that the money can be paid directly into your account. However, in the attack below the bank account details don't add anything for the attacker. So here is the attack:

1. 'Thank you, can I ask you how long you have been using telephone banking?'

2. 'What is the main reason you like telephone banking?'

3. 'How often to you call your online bank?'

4. 'Tell me, which bank do you use and how do you rate your bank on a scale of 1 to 10, where 10 is the best?'

5. 'What salary bracket do you fit into, less than £20k, £20k–£40k or £40k+?'

6. 'Do you use an overdraft facility on your telephone banking: never, regularly, sometimes?'

7. 'Thank you, that is the end of the questions. Thanks for your help. The last step is to enter you into our £500 prize draw. There is a winner picked every day. I just need to take your full name, first line of your address and your postcode. If you win a cheque will be posted to you in the morning.'

Of course the target information is gained in questions 4 and 7.

The critical question here is to obtain the name of the bank (quicker than going through rubbish bins, although this does give the attacker the bank, name and address). The question is 'hidden' in the middle of the questions and also makes up only the first part of the question to help hide it with something that requires more conscious processing (thinking of what score to give the bank). In addition, the question has a 'tell me' instruction to the subconscious preceding it.

The second part of the information is obtained in question 7 (after telling the target the lie 'that is the end of the questions', a useful technique for getting someone's guard down). The posting of the cheque is a justification for wanting full name and the address details. These are useful as they often form part of the authentication details the target's bank will want. In addition, they can be used for the initial call to the target when pretending to be the bank, adding some authenticity to the call.

The telephone survey has a second advantage, it allows the attacker to ascertain which individuals are more likely to give out information to a caller they cannot authenticate the identity of.

Having got a list of individuals, the banks they currently use and their addresses, the next task for the attacker is to work out the authentication details used by banks for the telephone banking service. This can be achieved by opening accounts and trialling the service. This has another advantage in that the attacker would also learn which banks routinely call their customers and in what way they ask for authentication details in this process. Thus, making the attacks more convincing to the target.

So what are the systemic improvements that could be implemented by the banks to counter this type of attack?

Systemic improvements:

- Two-factor authentication. The current most widespread application of this technique is the hardware token with an electronic display with a number that changes periodically (typically every 30 or 60 seconds). This number is typed in at the time of access, usually alongside the username and password. As this ever changing number is time synchronized with the system being accessed, you must have physical access to the device to login as the user. Therefore, the attacker must steal the device, in addition to stealing the user credentials. Or get the user to divulge their login details AND current token readout over the phone. The attacker then instantly enters them into the system – quite possible to achieve, so don't think the hardware token is impossible to bypass. Another variation is a second piece of authentication information that is sent via an SMS text message to the user's mobile phone as they attempt to login, again the principle here is that the attacker would have to obtain the user's mobile phone in addition to possessing their login credentials.

- Authentication of the caller. The bank should not ask for authentication if calling the person and instead allow banking users to call the operator back. This bad practice is common with many banks and opens the door to attackers targeting their customers. This doesn't stop an attacker making a call unless the customer has the clear understanding that the bank will never call them and ask for any details. A much better system for the bank is to call the customer and ask them to call the number on the back of their credit/cash card. However, this does require that the banks' telephone systems facilitate directing incoming calls to their call centre operators, something that is often not the case with multiple (often outsourced) operations.

ATTACK TWO – TELEPHONE ATTACK TO GAIN CONFIDENTIAL DOCUMENT

This attack, again using the telephone, is targeted at an organization holding confidential documents. The goal is to get the target to release information in one of two ways:

- email, if the document is held electronically;
- facsimile, if the document is on paper.

This is a classic social engineering attack, conducted at a distance in a way that avoids detection. The destination email can be set up remotely, either using a public webmail system or a hacked email server. The fax machine could be within another target organization which has been primed to forward it on to the final destination (they are very unlikely to keep a record of the number that it is forwarded to). In both instances it is quite likely that the attacker can carry out the attack without leaving a trail of evidence that can be used to identify them.

The attacker needs the following information to launch the attack:

- The identification of the target document – it is no good just knowing that you store sensitive information on the latest takeover deal. The attacker needs to identify precisely which document they are targeting if they are going to request it be sent to them in a convincing way.
- The identification of a relevant employee who has access to the document.

In general, this type of attack often has an insider element. A person who can identify the document and know who has access to it. Otherwise, the caller would normally have to conduct some extensive remote surveillance to gather sufficient organizational information to identify the target document and the person who can retrieve it for them.

Systemic improvements:

- Classification of information. This is a fundamental of information protection, allowing users to easily identify which information is sensitive. It is no coincidence that the military have a long history of its use.

- Associated information handling rules. The classification system itself is of limited value without clear rules related to each classification. If applied correctly, this reduces employees' subjectivity in knowing which documents they can release.

- Logical access controls. As you don't want to completely rely on staff understanding and application of information handling rules, where possible you should build in access controls that enforce the handling rules and help prevent staff from breaking those rules. For example, if only the senior partners in a law firm have authorization to access critical court documents for a given case, then electronic access should be restricted to just those individuals.

- Segregation of duties could also be applied in this scenario. For example, if information within the highest level of classification requires official sign-off from a senior manager before release, then this places a potential check (and barrier) between the user and the attacker. Although it can be relatively time consuming, this process is appropriate for handling high-value information that can only be released under exceptional circumstances.

ATTACK THREE – PHYSICAL ACCESS TO OFFICE AND SECURE AREAS

This could be to disrupt operations, remove equipment, install equipment or gain access to information.

Being on-site, this attack carries with it a higher level of personal risk for the attacker. However, with most CCTV cameras currently unable to accurately identify individuals, the risks could be lower than you think. Also, in our experience, when challenged, attackers usually manage to make a swift exit without being caught. This is especially the case when you consider that preventing an attacker from leaving could place the challenger under personal physical risk, and therefore wouldn't normally be advised.

The attacker needs the following information to launch the attack:

- Information regarding the external perimeter access controls – this is often achieved with a simple perimeter walk, combined with observation of the workings of the reception access controls and any delivery areas.

- Internal location of sensitive information – this can be more of a challenge without some insider knowledge. Having said that, once an attacker has gained access to a given organization, the location details are often quite easy to find within departments.

- Internal access controls – this can be observed if having previously accessed the building (as a visitor for example), or with insider information.

Systemic improvements:

- Classification of information. As with the previous example, the classification of information is the starting point in establishing effective physical access protection.

- Implementation of secure areas. The aim here is to set up internal zones, with physical entry controls similar to those you would expect on the perimeter of the organization. These could be electronic access control mechanisms such as swipe cards or PIN entry codes, or if appropriate internal reception/guarding points with 24/7 staffing.

The use of secure zones should be supported by clear rules regarding access by different personnel. For example, visitors would be limited to exterior zones, the majority of staff allowed further, with only a small number of essential people allowed within the confidential zones.

It is worth noting (and analysing within your risk assessment) that once your physical protection is of sufficient strength, the attacker's attention will switch to electronic or other remote social engineering attack vectors.

It is interesting to see the extensive physical security countermeasures often deployed around data centres (and used as selling points for prospective customers), whilst the main attack vector for these installations is electronic attack via the Internet.

ATTACK FOUR – EMAIL PHISHING ATTACK TO GAIN USERNAME AND PASSWORD TO HUMAN RESOURCES SYSTEM

In this example, the Human Resources (HR) system has been outsourced to a third party and is available as on online, Internet facing, service.

This attack is aimed at gathering personal information, held on the HR system within a database. The information present on such systems often includes name, date of birth, address, national insurance number (for the United Kingdom) and bank account details (as the system often allows users to change their designated bank account for salary payments). Additional information could also include employee salary and tax details, benefit schemes, holiday bookings, and so on.

The attacker is using access to gather enough personal information to enable identity theft. In addition, the access may be enough to launch more technical attacks against the application to gain access to more information than that available to a single user.

The attacker needs the following information to launch the attack:

- Internet address of the target system – this is made easy by:

    i) the nature of the Internet
    ii) the way that 'software as a service' applications are usually deployed.

- Identification of users – as this is usually all employees within the same organization, it is not too difficult to obtain.

- Email addresses of users – this is often a simple combination of firstname.lastname@companydomain, so easily obtained, or even guessed.

In addition, this attack (without being combined with other technical hacking techniques) relies on the HR system being Internet facing.

Systemic improvements:

- Remove the system from the Internet – by far the biggest factor in reducing risk, as this reduces the potential attack population from millions to perhaps a few hundred. However, this massive reduction in risk comes at a price – functionality. Rather than have the convenience of accessing your personal details from a web café, or any other Internet connection, you would restrict access to only work from the employer's office. The ideal would be to have the system actually hosted at the employer's site. However, a compromise would be to keep the system located on the Internet and to restrict access by Internet IP address so that only access from a designated range of addresses would be allowed.

• Use of two-factor authentication for access, as in example attack one above, this would involve users requiring a second authentication mechanism over and above information that they know, currently this is usually a hardware token.

• Stop publicizing the system. It is common practice for providers of these hosted (software as a service) applications to publicize the clients using them. This tends to be through two mechanisms:

i)   case study, client list and other marketing information on their website;

ii) information leakage due to sloppy security coding of their web application. This publicity opens the door to attacks originating from routine hacker surveillance of the system provider, or attacks directed at the outsourcing organization where background research on the Internet identifies the link to the hosted site.

Social Engineering Model of Protection

As you can see in the examples above, many of the systemic improvements offer strong protection against social engineering. In many cases, these systems will withhold attack where a number of individuals have been successfully persuaded by the attacker to comply. The system prevents the tricked user into causing a breach.

Our analysis of systemic improvements still leads to the conclusion that they tend to offer a stronger, and more consistent, layer of defence than simple staff awareness activities. Therefore we use the model shown in Figure 10.1 to illustrate this concept.

As you can see in Figure 10.1, we regard the staff awareness and associated reaction to be the first, and most important, layer of defence. However, our assumption is that this layer will be breached, potentially on a regular basis for

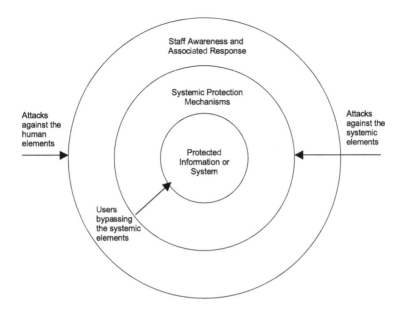

Figure 10.1 Social engineering model of protection

high-value information. Therefore, relying only on this protection mechanism is a high-risk strategy, leaving your information and systems vulnerable to attack.

The second, and more important layer, is the systemic protection that prevents staff who have been successfully persuaded by the attacker from actually carrying out a compromise of the protected information. Therefore, to build effective defences, you need to combine layers of staff awareness with systemic protection layers. We assume that neither layer is impenetrable.

Mapping Attack and Protection Combinations

By mapping attacks on to the proposed model, a clear link is established between specific attack vectors and associated systemic protection countermeasures.

In the example mapping shown in Figure 10.2, I have documented two attacks from the example attacks above:

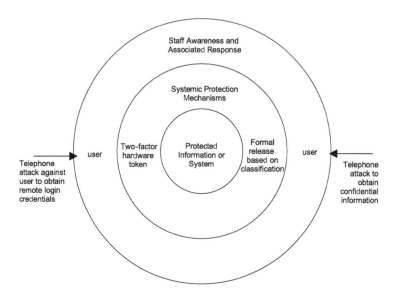

Figure 10.2 Mapping attacks and countermeasures to the model of protection

1.   A telephone attack against the user to obtain their login credentials
      is prevented by the two-factor hardware token.

2.   The telephone attack to directly obtain confidential information is
      made more difficult by the presence of a formal release procedure,
      linked to the classification of the target information.

Using this method you can effectively map attacks against the different layers
of defence and uncover situations where you are completely reliant on your
staff without the added benefit of systemic protection mechanisms.

STAFF ALERTS

An additional feature of members of staff is their ability to act as effective
Intrusion Detection Systems, giving early warning of attacks. The equivalent
feature in technical layers of defence can be complex to configure and manage
effectively.

This concept of using people for intrusion detection will be explored more
in the next chapter.

An additional consideration within the model is the ability of some users
to bypass the systemic elements of protection. These are often the system
administrators.

Although attacks against the majority of users can be effectively countered by the introduction of systemic protection, the administrators will usually carry the additional risk if they are successfully attacked.

The elevated privileges of systems administrators, and other individuals who may have the ability to bypass system protection layers, requires additional countermeasures. These may include extensive background checks and vetting, additional awareness and training and monitoring of their activities in order to alert security staff to any suspicious behaviour. This monitoring provides the added benefit of enabling the detection of insider attacks from this critical group.

Although systems administrators should possess additional knowledge of security, including social engineering, it should not be assumed that they are immune from attack. If the systemic protection layers can prevent users from assisting a social engineering attack, the system administrators become the only effective target for the attacker.

ATTACKING SYSTEMIC PROTECTION LAYERS

It is important to remember that within any system you will have certain individuals with more power. If they are successfully attacked, even the strongest systems can be bypassed. In addition, systems usually have avenues of technical attack that still need to be considered alongside the social engineering route. We know hackers will use whichever means gives them the desired results.

For example, if you look at the hardware token used for two-factor authentication it would appear to be very strong. (Assuming the attacker is remote, and not in a position to steal the token.) However, you often find vulnerabilities in the overall system when you investigate what a user does 'in an emergency', when they have lost their token. In our experience, it is not uncommon for the organization helpdesk to have a process that allows the user to call in, a new token is allocated, and (critically) the helpdesk then reads out the token value over the phone so the user can successfully login.

Clearly this situation lends itself to a social engineering attack against the helpdesk once the user's normal credentials are obtained. In order to predict that type of attack, you need to think like an attacker when designing any process that could potentially bypass a security countermeasure.

EXTENDED MODEL

The model can be further extended to look at the effect that the relatively public nature of the target information system has, and how much information is easily available to attract the attention of an attacker. A lack of publicly available information about a system can act as another layer of protection, as shown in Figure 10.3.

As you will understand, the more information that leaks into the public domain then the easier an attacker's task becomes in formulating a social engineering approach. The barriers in this layer also extend to how difficult it could be for an attacker to gather this information. You should regard not only the critical information to be the target, but also details of how they are protected to be useful to an attacker.

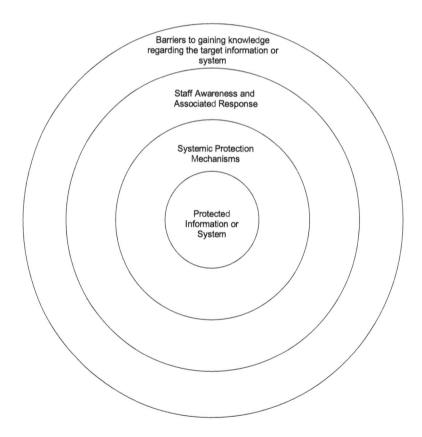

Figure 10.3 Extending the social engineering model of protection

PROTECTING THE PUBLICITY OF YOUR CRITICAL INFORMATION AND SYSTEMS

Developing an effective culture where information is only shared when strictly necessary is a good starting point for keeping details of systems from the attention of an attacker.

Being careful with information put into the public domain, and monitoring information appearing on the Internet, can be very valuable to your system security. For example, you can set up alerts with some search engines that will generate an email when information is discovered on the Internet relating to key words. If you set these up to include important words, such as your organization name, you can effectively detect information going into the public domain. This may include case studies from suppliers or system details getting posted by technical staff in an online forum.

There are many situations when details of your critical information and systems will be known (at the very least to your current and previous employees), and we are aware of the weaknesses of people. Therefore, the systemic layer is the most crucial in guaranteeing the security of your systems from social engineering attack.

There are some systemic protection mechanisms, that give you the greatest benefits:

INFORMATION CLASSIFICATION

Here we will work on the premise that the social engineer attacker is looking to obtain information. If we are to establish levels of protection around key information, then an information classification system can form the basis of developing effective countermeasures.

In our experience, leaving decisions as to what information can and cannot be shared down to each individual's judgement is opening the door to social engineers to extract your sensitive information.

At ECSC we have undertaken many consultancy projects helping people to develop their Information Security Management System (ISMS) to gain certification to ISO 27001 (formerly BS 7799).

Some ISO 27001 certifications can sometimes be paper exercises to get the certificate with the least amount of effort, especially where very limited scopes do not match the genuine information security risks of the organization. This is usually when the certification is needed to gain a contract, without any other drivers to improve security. However, more often than not, a certified ISMS will bring significant improvements to security.

The inclusion of a classification system is usually regarded as essential in an ISMS, although strictly speaking only as an optional control, and we have come across a small number of certifications that have decided not to implement one.

In our experience, the formation of a workable classification system can have many benefits, helping to formalize the necessary information handling rules that form the basis of the ISMS, and in particular form the backbone of social engineer protection.

For those people who have limited experience of operating under an information classification system, given that their historical application has been restricted mainly to government and military, we shall construct a simple system to illustrate the process.

We usually find that organizations, even when declaring no classification system exists, have a range of informal classifications and associated handling practices. In one example, a client who needed to establish an ISO 27001 certified ISMS insisted that they had no labels for identification of sensitive information. However, a simple text search of their existing quality manuals (certified to ISO 9001) showed use of the following: secret, confidential, company confidential, restricted, personnel in confidence, strictly confidential and sensitive. These were just the words used within their formal documentation and they didn't think they were classifying information. How could their staff be expected to understand what needed protecting and how to protect it?

In our logical starting point for a classification system, we shall begin with only three levels. For organizations with very little previous experience using information classification this is a good starting point. One of the common mistakes we find is when people try to invent too many levels in their classification scheme, resulting in too much complexity. Even simple systems need care in the introduction to get staff understanding and buy in.

There are a variety of classification labels you can use; the ISO 27001 standard doesn't dictate labels or the number of levels. One issue that you should be aware of is the potential overlap, or conflict, with another organization's classified information that you may exchange. At ECSC, we add the company name to the classification label. So 'ECSC – RESTRICTED' can be distinguished from other people's classification labels. For example, we also handle UK government 'RESTRICTED' information.

So our example three levels, with simple definitions are:

- Secret – information of particular value, with access restricted to small number of defined individuals.

- Company Confidential – routine organizational information, normally restricted to employees, contractors and 'trusted' third parties.

- Public – information suitable for dissemination to anyone.

These levels are a good starting point. Our advice, depending upon your organization's current position, is to start with something similar and review its operation to see if it needs adaptation.

A good rule of thumb:

- If your handling rules are very similar for two different classifications, then consider consolidating them into one single classification level to reduce complexity.

- If you need different subrules for handling different information within the same classification, then consider expanding your system with a new level of classification.

With a system such as above, you could expect the quantity of information to be something like:

- Secret – 15 per cent.

- Company Confidential – 70 per cent.

- Public – 15 per cent.

Clearly, the exact proportions will depend upon your organization, its operations, reliance on information confidentiality and its public facing information flows. However, you can work on the principle that a relatively small amount of information is suitable for public dissemination and a similarly small quantity requires special levels of protection over and above the usual organizational perimeter.

With increasing reliance upon efficient communication and sharing of information beyond the traditional organizational boundaries, it is important that a classification system does not constrain operations beyond that necessary to support an appropriate level of security.

With a clearly defined classification system and a workable way of identifying the classification of each piece of information, you can then begin to define appropriate rules for the sharing of information.

For example, you could develop rules for the faxing of information relating to our new three-level classification system:

Classification level	Use of fax
Secret	Not allowed
Company Confidential	Only to known recipients
Public	No restrictions

These simple guidelines can then be disseminated to staff to help protect against the leak of information to a social engineer who could trick someone into faxing a document to them.

EXECUTIVE AND SENIOR MANAGEMENT SUPPORT

Now for anyone who has tried to establish working information handling rules, and especially for any senior managers reading this, it is worth looking at the problems that can be created without the proper support by senior people.

At worse, policies and procedures for the protection of information are treated by senior managers as a set of rules for everyone else. 'Being so important, and so intelligent, they don't need to be constrained by these inflexible rules.' However, it is exactly that weakness that will be exploited by the social engineer. If your authority allows you to bypass the rules, then an attacker only needs to assume the same level of authority and everyone capitulates into allowing them the access necessary to steal your information.

The answer is quite simple – everyone follows the rules. If the rules are not right for senior managers, then they need to be improved and adapted until they are right for everyone.

In our example above, if a senior manager were to bully someone into faxing them a secret document against the information security rules, then they should be disciplined. Under no circumstances should anyone ever be disciplined for following the rules.

Now you may be thinking, 'There could be some circumstances, where I forget something, and need it faxing to me in an emergency.' In that case, create a suitable exception, such as:

'In exceptional cases, secret documents may be faxed by members of the senior team. In such cases, the PA to the CEO must be informed of the circumstances.'

This allows senior management an exception, whilst creating a record of their use of it.

This leads us neatly to another critical area:

EXECUTIVE INFORMATION

It has long been our observation, within many organizations that I come across, that there has been a drastic reduction in the security of executive-level information with the introduction of new 'improved' information and communications technologies.

Please let your mind go back to before the wave of new technology swept most organizations and imagine the chief executive, situated in the heart of the executive block, guarded by a pretty fierce secretary. She may even have had a good old fashioned typewriter.

Not only was she (and she almost certainly would have been a she) there to support, she was also an excellent access control mechanism. Information generated within the executive area largely remained their under lock and key. With their own filing systems, and local document control, release of information could be, and usually was, controlled.

Contrast that with the situation in most modern organizations. Although there are still some older individuals who keep to this old way of working, most senior people are busy typing their own documents, and communicating, using the corporate IT system. This is the system that places all their information under the direct control of the IT department, not their trusted secretarial staff. For many organizations this means that even the most junior members of the IT helpdesk can access the most 'confidential' documents of the executives. A risk either unknown, or ignored, by senior managers, and certainly not in the interest of the IT department to fully explain to anyone.

This of course gives the social engineer an ideal direct route to some of the most business critical information within your organization – through the helpdesk. The very people you train to be as helpful as possible, especially if a senior manager needs something urgently. Let's say, for example, they are away on a business trip and need something emailing out to them that they have forgotten. They don't have access to remote email, so you will have to send it to that other 'trusted' address they supplied you with.

I am sure you can see the scenario building, and how the social engineer can exploit these inherent systemic weaknesses in your organization.

It is my view, that for many organizations, the segmentation of IT systems to facilitate the physical separation of distinct categories of information is not widespread enough. In many instances it is not only appropriate, however, but also quite feasible to provide senior executives with completely separate managed systems to ensure that their own IT staff cannot gain access to business critical confidential documents.

There have been quite a few occasions when we have been called out to investigate incidents where it is clear that the IT staff have been routinely reading a variety of senior executive documents and 'private' communication. At some stage they have given away the fact that they knew something that could only have been learnt by interception of communication, or accessing files without authorization.

Access Controls

The world of IT is now recognizing that it must go beyond passwords, using two-factor authentication such as biometrics or tokens. Even the UK banks are now recognizing that online banking with only a username and password is just too open to exploit by a variety of attackers.

However, in many cases, your authentication of verbal access is 'zero-factor' authentication as it requires no evidence to verify identity. We can use the benefits of the information classification scheme to define conditions under which information can be disclosed verbally. Many of our clients are now establishing rules for verbal communication. For example, using our previous simple classification scheme, you could start with something like:

Classification level	Verbal Communication
Secret	Within designated 'secure areas' and private areas
Company Confidential	On company premises and non-public areas
Public	No restrictions

So, for example, discussion in the car going to a meeting would be okay for all levels. However, a busy airport lounge would only be appropriate for public information.

As your awareness of social engineering vulnerabilities becomes more acute, you will notice more and more areas of risk. You will, no doubt, start to find other people's mobile phone conversations on public transport more interesting than annoying.

In one recent example, simply by using my ears on a train journey, I managed to glean the name of a company who had just won a contract to supply drinks to a large pub chain in an area of the UK. Although this was a massive win for them, they had lied in the tender and in fact couldn't fulfil a major requirement of the contract – the supply of wines. They now had only weeks to find someone to step in and help them. I also had the name and mobile number of the individual who had allowed me to listen to his admission of this information to a colleague.

Now armed with this, I could have either made sure their customer was aware of their dishonesty or exploited their relative desperation and offer to help them on very favourable terms. I could have simply offered to sell this valuable information to a competitor or even offered them the option of buying my silence. So many options with just a few minutes of talking in a public place without thinking about the consequences.

Incident: Free Money

Have you ever wondered how to get free money at the race track? Perhaps not, however, someone such as Derren Brown has a mind that works that way. Although this exploit was performed as part of one of his television shows, I have included it as an incident, as it highlights perfectly the vulnerabilities that can be exploited to trick someone into performing a, seemingly crazy, action.

The location is Walthamstow Stadium, a dog racing track where people bet on animals running after a imitation rabbit. As with all betting establishments, it is owned by someone very rich and attended by plenty of people who are very poor.

The intention in this exercise is to get the lady in the kiosk to pay out winnings on a losing ticket. How is this achieved? Well, at a simple level, by asking her to, however with a few other little tricks thrown in.

Kiosk one

The words used in the first example, approaching the kiosk with a losing ticket for the last race, initially delivered by a 'punter' working with Derren:

'This is the winning ticket!'

A key aspect is to look the lady in the eye, and believe that you have a winning ticket. By believing that the ticket is a winning ticket, your body language will match the other people collecting winnings – a simple mind script will help.

When the operator doesn't look as if she is going to pay, Derren bangs the palm of his hand against the side of the kiosk window, in effect creating an interrupt like the handshake interrupt, together with the words.

'This is the dog you're looking for!'

Designed to give the suggestion that she has found what she is looking for, that is, the winning ticket.

'Try again, you may have misread it.'

She then apologizes for her mistake, saying, 'Sorry, yes, you have won, sorry,' and proceeds to pay out £109.

Kiosk two

On the second occasion, some interesting variations are tried:

'This is the winning ticket!', as in the first example.

The operator checks, and returns the ticket saying, 'Sorry, this didn't win.' Derren responds with another bang on the kiosk and, as above,

'This is the dog you're looking for. It's why we came to this window!'

After a further check, she agrees and pays out on the losing ticket. The magic of the last phrase was the extra emphasis placed on the WIN in 'window', placing a word directly into the subconscious, hidden within a reasonable and logical statement.

A really interesting comment was made by the lady when her error was pointed out to her. After initial confusion, her conscious brain did its best to find a rational explanation for her action, and the best she could come up with was:

'He just told me to pay out!'

The irony of the sign saying 'no mistakes can be rectified after leaving window' was not lost on the participants.

Vulnerability analysis

The ladies working within the betting kiosks were vulnerable on a number of fronts:

- They are doing a repetitive job, therefore they will get bored, their conscious mind wandering, with the task in hand dropping into the subconscious.

- How many times had they been asked to payout on a losing ticket? Probably never, although perhaps a few times since Derren's exploits were shown on television.

Possible countermeasures

- Testing, in this circumstance, if the operators had previously been tested in a similar way, they would then be working much more at a conscious level, looking for possible repeat tests.

- Systemic changes that require the operator to input something from the winning ticket to confirm a win. Although, I suspect in this case the operators were going against the official process in making a payment.

AREN'T BIOMETRICS THE ANSWER?

Within the EU, the biometrics industry has recently received a boost with the ePassport requiring two finger images for each individual. The UK national identity database currently plans to go further with data from ten fingerprints, two iris scans and the facial shape.

Additional emerging technologies include:

- Voice recognition – matching tonal characteristics to pre-recorded templates.

- Hand geometry – the dimensions and overall shape of the whole hand.

- Hand veins – using infrared imaging to measure the internal vein structure of the hand.

- Signature – in addition to the shape, measuring pressure and velocity data as you sign.

- Keystroke dynamics – measuring the characteristics of your typing rate and intervals.

So a whole range of ideas and technologies that promise the demise of the password could make the life of a social engineer more of a challenge. However, if we put our 'sceptical of vendors of technology solutions' hat on, we may be more cautious in our optimism.

If you like crime and spy movies, you may be led to believe that biometrics are commonplace in the high-tech world of espionage and secret government installations. The technology may enhance a movie, however, in reality, their use within the military to date has been virtually non-existent.

Let's explore the best known biometric technology to illustrate the difference in reality to our 'beliefs' – fingerprint recognition. You may well have seen in CSI or similar police dramas the computer rapidly scanning through a massive database of fingerprints to identify the suspect. It even usually shows many images flash past on screen to show the viewer something whilst it works!

The reality – in Clarksburg, West Virginia, the FBI employs around 2200 *humans* to analyse up to 50 000 prints per day.

Yes, supported by 80 terabytes of computing. But the final matching still has to be done by the human operator.

The current technology just isn't good enough to deliver what we see in fiction, particularly when you use the technology on large groups of individuals.

HACKING BIOMETRICS

So how do you go about hacking biometrics? We will explore three attack vectors, as shown in Figure 10.4, to help you understand that these systems are not without vulnerabilities and therefore still open to security threats.

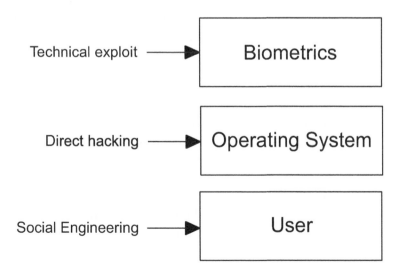

Figure 10.4 Hacking attack vectors for biometric systems

TECHNICAL EXPLOIT

The biometric systems themselves often have a range of vulnerabilities that allow direct attack. For example, a little-known technique for bypassing fingerprint readers involves the user of jelly babies to lift the last impression from the reader and then use it to gain access. Other more complex techniques can exploit the internal encryption and transmission mechanisms of the biometric data to compromise the system.

DIRECT HACKING

An important area often overlooked is that biometric systems are often built upon the same insecure operating systems. Therefore, all the traditional network-based hacking techniques can be used to access the data. Sometimes the hacker isn't even aware that a biometric system was in place as they simply access the data directly.

SOCIAL ENGINEERING

Of course users of biometric systems still have the same human vulnerabilities that make social engineering attacks so effective. Therefore accessing data or disrupting systems through trickery, persuasion and forced error is still an effective way to bypass the new authentication technology. You can simply let the target use their biometrics to access the system and then manipulate them into performing the actions you wish.

We must also remember that when describing alternative approaches such as the three above, that attackers will choose the weakest link. In addition, they will freely move between attack types and combine them where necessary: whatever it takes to achieve their goal.

One of the major risks with the inevitable introduction of biometrics is the misplaced trust in their accuracy, as demonstrated in the recent case of a police officer, Ms McKie, in Scotland. An unquestioning belief in an identification system, in this case traditional fingerprints, can lead to major incidents of injustice.

In this example fingerprint 'experts' were asked to confirm whether a sample (Ms McKie) fingerprint matched those taken at the scene of the crime. The reply that came back was that they did. This result was also replicated by another 'expert'.

After a long battle to prove her innocence, Ms McKie successfully showed that there was not a valid match. What was surprising was that the results of subsequent fingerprint matching not only showed that the original identification was suspect, but that the two sets of fingerprints did not match very well at all. In fact, they were very poor matches.

So why did a well-established and trusted 'biometric' system fail? There are two factors at play here:

- Firstly, there is a belief that fingerprint identification is to be trusted and that experts in the field do not get things wrong.

- Secondly, and perhaps more interestingly, is the concept of using fingerprints to confirm a match, rather than finding a match.

The second point is worth exploring. Let's say you have your crime scene fingerprints and you send them away to be matched, perhaps against a million known criminals on file.

In this case the result will be to the question:

Which of the million known fingerprints is the best match to the crime scene?

Here the expert will be finding the best match, looking at a number of features.

In the case of Ms McKie, a very different question was asked, namely:

Does this single fingerprint match the crime scene?

In this case there is not a pool of fingerprints to choose from, only one to 'try and match'. The incentive for the analyst is to find a match. They looked for reasons to confirm the match and then duly found them.

When someone working for Ms McKie's defence, with a belief in her innocence, looked for reasons why they didn't match, they also found many reasons to confirm their belief.

So how could this fingerprinting exercise have been conducted in a more objective way? Simply Ms McKie's fingerprints should have been added to the millions of records currently available, and a normal search conducted to see if she was the best match. In that way, no beliefs of her guilt, or incentive to help the investigation, could have come into play. In effect, the search would have been blind to her identity, and her records would not have had any undue priority in the search.

This should serve as a warning in the trust of biometrics to give 100 per cent accuracy. We are in the infancy of this technology and have a long way to go before we can trust the results it gives us.

Awareness and Training

Our aims with social engineering security awareness and training are two-fold:

1. Raise awareness of the threat from social engineering attack, to increase the likelihood of an attack being detected and thwarted.

2. Train users to comply with and support the systemic security countermeasures that protect information and systems from attack.

To begin with, I would like to outline some of the many and varied awareness building activities that our clients use, often with our help. Many of these apply in general to information security, the social engineering element of protection will depend upon the specific protection countermeasures that you have developed within this framework.

Awareness-Building Activities

INDUCTION TRAINING

Most organizations, assuming even a most basic approach to information security, will have elements of awareness and training in their induction programme for new staff. This may be a quick add-on to their IT induction or something which is part of the general procedures, including physical security routines.

Clearly, it is important to induct new staff and establish the important elements of their new work environment that they need to be aware of. Unfortunately, in many organizations, their information security awareness and training doesn't extend beyond a quick session for new staff in their first week.

It is important to remember, that when entering a new organization as an employee, you are often bombarded with information from numerous departments. Whilst appearing to be keen to learn, the sheer volume of content lessens that longer-term impact. Most employees will quickly learn over the first few weeks the elements that are really important by observing the colleagues and quizzing them on 'what do I need to know?' Many induction programmes gather dust on people's shelves.

Having pointed out the negatives, it is important to ensure that information security is adequately covered for new entrants. An increasing number of employees will have worked under Information Security Management Systems (ISMS) in their previous employment. Induction should be an opportunity to establish two simple outcomes:

1.   Yes, we also take security seriously here.

2.   These are the main elements you will need to be aware of.

I don't expect too much content to 'stick' in the mountain of other information supplied by 'competing' departments. Employees will be trying to work out what is important to them; my aim is to ensure that they are left with the impression that information security, including the social engineering elements, is one of these crucial categories.

These important messages will diminish in their effectiveness unless you sustain them with follow-on activities.

FACE-TO-FACE BRIEFINGS

Getting a group of employees together for a face-to-face, interactive training session is one of the most effective ways of developing your information security. This clearly assumes that the content is interesting and relevant and also that the delivery is entertaining, and critically, 'memorable'.

Having delivered many training sessions in this way, I can attest to the positive reaction from staff, and their thanks for the understanding they leave with. They are often particularly pleased with the elements of their own personal information security that they can improve with the content. I find hooking content into their personal security can be a good way to get their attention.

However, it is important to remember that, although potentially very effective, this type of awareness building is also quite resource intensive. The time taken to prepare effective materials, obtaining the right person to deliver this and, sometimes more critically, the cost in time for each person attending, mean this method should be used intelligently.

Also, because individuals are often 'giving their time' to attend, if this isn't done well then it can set back any efforts to gain support for information security initiatives. I am sure you will remember training that you have loved and also training that wasted your time.

EMAIL BULLETINS

Many people are making use of email as a cost-effective mechanism for delivering information security messages. Whilst it certainly can be cheap it has two main drawbacks:

1.   The number of people who actually read it can be very low.

     Clearly this depends on the volume of other messages they receive. In general, I prefer to be able to track who has received the message, with some ability to measure the success. To try and gauge likely success, I like to sit with some typical users and understand the quantity and quality of the internal email communications they receive. This is time well spent before deciding if this is going to be an effective mechanism for delivering critical content.

2.   You could be opening social engineering vulnerabilities.

     This method could be establishing the precedent that email instructions from the information security team are to be followed. A social engineer getting sight of these emails could use them to spoof a less welcome communication to socially engineer their target. You need to question whether a communication method that can be used by an outsider is the right choice to deliver your, sometimes critical, information.

     You only have to look at the quite common fake information security alerts that are circulated within organizations, often by well-meaning staff. On occasions they helpfully instruct users to search for, and delete, malicious files on their PC; the attack being to get users to delete essential files, therefore creating a denial of service attack.

You can take measures to manage the two issues above. For example, there are well-established mechanisms for tracking who opens emails, with a number of systems that will track when and how often people have read your communication.

In addition, you can filter incoming email and internal communication to identify potential social engineering content that is trying to duplicate your valid messages.

INTRANET POSTINGS

Whilst the intranet can be a useful and quickly accessed source of information, the same concern exists in getting people to access it, and tracking their activity can have limitations.

Again, as with emails communication, there are systems that will allow you to track activity and relate this to individual users. Unfortunately, when established, many of these tracking systems can just train users that they have to 'visit' the information in order to satisfy the tracking; it may not be showing you evidence of effective awareness building and training.

Having said that, the intranet is an effective place to store reference material in an easily accessible way. Where you have large groups of employees that need to have access to information, it can have its place.

INTERACTIVE ONLINE TRAINING

With the requirement to raise awareness and train large numbers of staff, a number of interactive online training packages focused on information security are emerging. These can have the advantage of directing content at large groups and also tracking usage. In many cases, these also offer an element of testing to confirm understanding. However, there are some serious limitations:

- Often the 'testing' comes directly after the content, whilst the material is still in short-term memory. This gives little indication of the longer-term retention of real levels of understanding.

- The independent nature of the training gives opportunities for individuals to cheat, either by directly accessing the materials at the same time as the test (using two logins for example) or by allowing someone else to complete the test for them.

- These systems are often shared with other departments, with everyone loading their content. An average user can be overwhelmed with training that they need to complete. Hence they look for strategies to satisfy the requirements with the least effort.

There is little that can compete with seeing the look on someone's face and the change when they grasp a concept, confirmed by their intelligent questions and comments. However, if you have an employee base of thousands that need to be covered then these systems have a place in your training armoury. It may be that this minimal coverage is still much better than your current situation.

LOGIN SCREEN MESSAGES

I am now seeing a number of clients using the login screen to deliver information security messages. Whilst not giving any guarantees of who will read them, if they are designed to grab attention and changed with some frequency then they can be effective.

You should, in light of the material within these pages, also consider the subconscious effect of messages displayed in this way. These messages can be an effective route to the subconscious. As these are repeated, the conscious brain quickly ignores them, yet the subconscious continues to absorb the message. A reread of the section on subconscious communication would be well worth your time before writing these, for example, you should remember that:

> 'Don't share your password' does contain the instruction 'share your password'. If this is delivered consistently then it will have an effect on some people. Better to use 'keep your password secure' as a positive message, not requiring the conscious brain to interpret the negative logic.

POSTERS

The subliminal potential of login screen messages can also be duplicated with the use of posters or other displays around the organization. You need to be careful if these are visible to visitors. However, by this stage, I am assuming your well-developed information classification system and use of secure areas and internal segregation will help you in this regard.

These sources of awareness building also have the effect of reminding people that the organization is placing great importance on security.

TESTING AND RELATED ACTIVITIES

I consider proper testing of information security, including social engineering, and other interactive activities to be amongst the best awareness building and training mechanisms. However, as with face-to-face training, they can be resource intensive. In limited, targeted, situations they can deliver big gains. These will be covered in more depth in the next chapter.

Another area to consider, in addition to larger testing programmes, is the use of smaller and regular testing activities. I have been involved in projects where these are conducted in the form of regular calls to people, where success in reporting the call to the information security team leads to a modest prize for the employee. Those that fall for the social engineering test are told about the test and reminded of the relevant training and information security procedures.

LOCAL CHAMPIONS

For larger organizations, the use of local information security champions can also be very effective. You may not be able to rely on all line managers playing an active role in information security development. However, you can often get interest and support from others within each team to act as the local information security representative.

This allows you to concentrate your awareness and training efforts on the champions and they can disseminate the information locally. They can also play a role in auditing compliance to information security policy and procedure, giving you valuable feedback.

In addition, this approach is integrating security into the more 'business as usual' and line manager activities.

Targeting Awareness and Training

You should note (as seen from the approach in the previous chapter) that there are situations where good compliance with systemic security protection can reduce the need for too much awareness raising.

It would be easy for me to tell you that everyone in your organization needs to be focusing on security, as most security professionals would agree. However, I have a few words of caution:

I am reminded of my (very valuable) studies for my Masters in Business Administration (MBA). The marketing specialist said, 'You need to ensure that everyone in the organization thinks about marketing.' Also, the Human Resource expert stressed how, 'Every manager needs to be a Human Resource manager.' Then the sales guru would tell us, 'You need to get everyone thinking like a salesperson.'

It is quite natural that we all think that the world would be a better place if everyone thought about, understood and supported our particular specialism. Of course this is not possible. We have to be realistic in our expectations of how much focus on security your average employee is able and willing to give you, and how much support from managers is achievable. In addition, if everyone spent too much time thinking about security that could well interfere with their ability to do their jobs.

Having realism in our expectations, combined with targeted approaches to training and awareness, is the best approach. As with any risk-based methodology, we target our activities where they will have the greatest impact in controlling the risks.

CATEGORIZING EMPLOYEES

So what level of training and awareness activities are appropriate for a given group of employees? The answer is 'the right amount'. This should be in proportion to the risks in their area of the organization.

Imagine if you were starting a job with the British Security Services (MI5). Perhaps day one may be a security briefing, and day two and perhaps day three! You may not even be that surprised if your first few weeks were helping you understand security procedures and the associated risks that you would have to keep in mind for the whole of your career in the service.

If you then had another day on updates each month, this would still not be excessive. Of course your focus on security is proportional to the level of threat and the potential impact of a security breach on your particular organization. This example is at an extreme.

Now, I am sure you can think of job functions in your organization (unless you work for MI5!) where this level of awareness and training would not be appropriate. To get senior management support we have to show the link between potential threat and likely impact, and the extent to which we will train individuals.

I am a firm believer in (where appropriate) starting an employee analysis with a simple high, medium and low categorization. So, for example you could think about a given organization's staff on this basis:

Employee category	Training and awareness	Access to critical information and/or systems
High	Regular, targeted and countermeasure specific	Direct access to critical information/systems
Medium	Induction and ongoing period updates	Potential access to critical information/systems
Low	Role specific instructions	No access to critical information/systems

This analysis would be linked to your specific information classifications. In the example above we have used the label 'critical' to indicate the most important information.

For employees in the 'Low' category, we don't give them any training or awareness activities as such, however, their role-specific instruction will include elements of security. For example, they may not be allowed to use the fax machine or may not have external email (or the rights to send attachments). These instructions and rules may not carry with them any in-depth understanding of security, however they do support the organization's policies and, if compliance is achieved, they will protect information.

This is in contrast to the employees in the 'High' category; they have direct access to critical information and systems and could do much more damage. As targets, they need to understand security to a higher level. You would provide these people with more regular training and awareness activities to raise their understanding and help them judge situations that may not have been explicitly covered in the standard training.

SYSTEMS ADMINISTRATORS

These are a special case, not recognized by most organizations as high risk, and worthy of some examination. The level of access to information and control of critical systems afforded to most systems administrators can cause us some difficulties with social engineering in relation to risk. They are particular targets for a skilled social engineering attacker looking for high returns.

Many people think that IT 'experts' are all particularly conscious of social engineering attacks and therefore don't need training. This is a big mistake. Firstly, it can be a serious error to assume that systems administrators are all experts in any field of information security, let alone a highly specialist one. Some are, yet many are not doing technically difficult roles, just roles that require administration-level access. Even highly technical does not mean security aware, and highly technical understanding could also be combined with very little understanding of human vulnerabilities. You probably know a few highly technical people with less than fully developed social skills.

It is important to recognize that in many IT systems, with inherently poor security architectures, too many people have full administration rights. If targeted successfully, these administrators can be very dangerous. In addition, these individuals can also end up being the source of attacks, either directly through their own intentions or under coercion of other manipulation.

Other factors can make training these individuals more difficult:

- People often find these technical people difficult to manage. Where they do have high-level skills, they often know more than their manager about the detail of their job.

- Administrators value their access, often they give themselves access beyond the level they really need. They will often have 'good' reasons for this, with few people in a position to challenge them.

- On occasions, a systems administrator can be quite powerful as they hold special knowledge that the organization needs to function.

A good strategy with systems administrators is to involve them in the design of a social engineering protection programme. Stroke their egos (even though they are often not this personality type) a little and motivate them to play an active role in building the appropriate defences.

On a few occasions I have advised senior managers that they have to build effective trust with these individuals or they have to remove them from the organization.

Social Engineering Awareness Building Strategies

You can think of social engineering awareness building as a four stage process:

STAGE ONE – CONSCIOUS AWARENESS OF THE THREAT

This can be through traditional face-to-face training, through a variety of online materials or through a mix of promotional 'advertising' of the security issues. Through delivering information security training to all levels within organizations, I can offer a few simple tips:

- Don't get too technical. Even in an audience of reasonably technical people, you will lose chunks of the audience very quickly. If you manage to help them understand something technical by explaining in a way that gives them new insight then you get results. However, looks of delight from some parts of the audience can hide the fact that you have just lost 30 per cent of them.

- Link the social engineering threats to their personal information. You can get a lot of interest by offering understanding and general advice to issues like identity theft and hacking home PCs. It is likely that your audience will be quite desperate for help in this area and it is useful to get their interest and attention.

- Aim to show them that the threat is real and related to their organization and area of activity. It can be okay to help them see that vulnerabilities can be complex and challenging to solve. This can be used to explain why rules are in place and, even though you may not understand why, it is important that they comply.

- Get senior managers to attend the training, not as a group but preferably along with other staff. There are some merits to training senior managers together (if you can get them together). However, the benefits to developing a security culture (see below) are greatly helped by their presence in routine training sessions.

STAGE TWO – BUILD A SECURITY CULTURE

The culture you need to support security is an interesting mix:

- you want your staff to comply with instructions (your security rules);

- you don't want your staff to comply with instructions (the social engineer's persuasion).

A fundamental of the ability to block social engineering attacks is the willingness of the target to challenge the attacker. It is of critical importance that people feel they can challenge for security-related issues without feeling they would be criticized in any way. This is easier said than done.

Challenging people, especially figures of perceived authority, is difficult as it goes against years of conditioning. Organizations are traditionally structured to give senior managers authority, power and control. Expecting an individual to challenge this (in certain circumstances) requires the right approach.

One key element here can be the explicit support of senior managers in attending training and confirming the support for staff who challenge when security rules or normal procedures are being bypassed. I often ask senior managers to attend training sessions with their staff just to give public confirmation that they are behind the initiative.

An effective route to allow staff to challenge is to give them a person to call when they feel uncomfortable challenging someone. This person (usually a security specialist) allows your employees to initiate the challenge yet not have to take full responsibility for any resulting actions. The escalation route for the team that deals with the challenge needs to extend to senior managers with enough perceived power to be able to counter other managers trying to bypass effective security.

STAGE THREE – ADD ALERTING TRIGGERS

Conscious triggers

Staff can be trained to look out for certain signs that a social engineering attack may be in progress. These triggers tend to be more effective for detecting the less skilled attacker, yet are still valuable in developing awareness of the threat:

- **Urgency** – an emergency is a good way to get actions that often bypass established process. Therefore, during an 'emergency' it is important to remind staff to carry out the 'what do I really know about this person?' test – separating out what the person has said from information confirmed from another source.

- **Authority** – using authority to bypass process is a dangerous activity to allow and something senior managers have a responsibility to keep to a minimum. A remote request, by whatever mechanism, with implied or explicit threats of authority should raise suspicion.

- **Strange requests** – a skilled attacker will have done enough research to be able to make any request appear to be business as usual. However, a less skilled attacker or someone in the early stages of information gathering may make strange requests or simply get things wrong in an unusual way. This could be the sign of an attack.

- **Name dropping** – excessive name dropping, trying a little too hard to prove that they really are part of the organization, can be a good clue to an attack in progress.

- **Being too nice** – a tricky one to distinguish from a nice person. However, most people can detect the difference between genuine and false niceness. Unfortunately, many people's subconscious will instantly decide to like the person, the overriding instinct may be to help them as much as possible.

As you can see, for every tactic developed by the social engineering attacker there is a potential trigger to detect the attack. However, the skill of the attacker needs to be matched by the skill of the target. Trying to get all your staff to be this informed and skilled is not realistic, hence our focus in the last chapter on developing more systemic protection to reduce the reliance upon individuals.

There are circumstances where you can invest extra effort and get the benefit from having a highly trained team. Perhaps you have a small amount of very confidential information protected by a dedicated, and valuable set of users. This is worth investing in. Or perhaps you have created a team to deal with suspicious requests and have a system of referrals based on triggers above. This can be a good strategy in a call centre operation, where widespread in-depth training is rarely cost-effective.

Subconscious triggers

It can be interesting to see how far you can take a team in their ability to deal with social engineering, especially if you take the psychology approach adopted in this book. Using the power of the subconscious in your defence can be interesting. For example:

Question: 'When do I call the security helpline?'

Answer: 'When you feel something is just not right.'

You may think this is rather strange advice. However, it does have its place. It has been observed that experts in a given field, with years of experience, develop a subconscious set of triggers that tell them when something is not right. They often cannot necessarily put it into words. So, when dealing with very experienced staff, say a receptionist with years of experience and in-depth knowledge of the organization, this can be good advice. Trusting your instincts has its place.

This is one reason why, when tricking receptionists into giving access during a social engineering test, if given a choice I am more likely to target the young (and therefore inexperienced) receptionist rather than the more experienced individual who may know 'something is not right'.

STAGE FOUR – TEST

To be covered in the next chapter in some depth. However, it is worth noting that testing programmes can be a good way of training staff in addition to the usual vulnerability identification and risk assessment focus.

COUNTER ATTACK

Why should information security be only about defence? It is an interesting question and worth examining in the context of social engineering attacks. As the attacker is, by the very nature of a social engineering attack, in 'personal' contact with the target, there is the opportunity to develop a reverse sting.

I remember, when phishing attacks first started to appear, working with a bank to design a counter attack strategy. This was based on early identification of servers hosting the fake bank sites and then making plenty of web requests of these servers. In effect, assuming the requests were made from suitably fast Internet connections, conducting a denial of service attack at the malicious site. The theory behind this strategy was that attacking an already compromised server would not 'harm' the target, as the owner would want to remove it from service anyway. In addition, the attack was a short-term measure designed to limit the losses of bank customers whilst the bank managed to have the system shut down by its hosting provider or owner.

So how do we extend the counter attack to a social engineering scenario? One method is to conduct a reverse sting. Simply put, a reverse sting is where you allow the attacker to think they are making progress with the attack whilst you direct them towards areas of your choice and gather information about them in the process.

For example, if you detect a phone-based social engineering attempt, you can 'helpfully' redirect the attack to specialists. The attacker can be made to think they are being put through to their intended target. In reality they are now speaking to someone trained to socially engineer them.

You can use this approach to learn more about the attacker, gathering information that can be helpful in preventing the attack leading to a serious breach. You can also, potentially, gather enough information to help investigations and future action against the attacker.

In my experience, attackers can have the same range of human vulnerabilities as anyone else. You can use this as the basis of the counter attack. For example, the attacker will be quite excited at the belief that they are making successful progress with their intended target. This belief that they are talking to someone else can cause them to give away unnecessary information.

For example, a social engineer 'caught' in this way, in the process of trying to socially engineer their target, tried to persuade someone to send a target piece of information in an email. The target, who was actually part of the information security incident response team, said 'yes' they would do that and asked for the email address. At this point the attacker would be getting quite excited at their imminent success and would not necessarily be thinking things through. When they supplied a public webmail address, the target informed them that their email system blocked such addresses. However, the document was there waiting to be sent and all they had to do was give them an alternative and they could send it. In the rush to get his intended target information, the attacker then gave an alternative email address (one that was subsequently used to identify him and, ultimately, the organization he was working for).

This simple example shows the power of the counter attack. If you can get the attacker to believe that they are making progress, you can direct them into situations where they divulge information or quite literally walk into a trap.

USE OF PEOPLE AS INTRUSION DETECTION SYSTEMS

I am a big fan of electronic Intrusion Detection Systems (IDS). They are often deployed without effective management and do not deliver the promised benefits. However, with the correct, expert, management they can transform your knowledge of your network security. Early detection of incidents is crucial for all sorts of information security attacks and social engineering attackers are no different.

Imagine that an attacker has made a call to a member of your call centre team to try and achieve a given attack and they are unsuccessful. What is stopping them immediately picking up the phone and trying to call another operator to try and find an easier target?

A common feature of many social engineering vulnerabilities, where systemic protection is lacking and people are the only defence, is that the attacker can have multiple targets to try as many times as they please until they are successful.

Therefore, you need to develop a way of turning a failed attack into a detected attack and take action as a result.

There are a number of components of such a human Intrusion Detection System:

- training and awareness of individuals to detect the attack;
- alerting mechanisms to report the attack in a timely fashion;
- pre-planned reaction to increase the levels of protection.

USE PERSUASION TO SUPPORT YOU

As you have explored the area of persuasion in this book and developed your skills in this area, you can begin to think about how you could deploy some of these techniques in helping your staff understand social engineering.

As an ethical professional, why not deploy some of your understanding to 'sell' the benefits of security and help your organization in a positive way? From conducting face-to-face training to designing awareness-building messages and briefing senior managers on the associated risks, you can use persuasion techniques to make your message more effective. This can be seen as no more than just being an effective communicator within your organization. You will probably find that as your personal awareness of persuasion techniques increases, you will use these techniques without consciously realizing it. You will also notice that the most effective communicators within your organization are using a variety of techniques, even if they do not realize it themselves.

Testing

Social engineering testing is often a new undertaking for many organizations.

In situations where there is no testing history to build upon, I usually recommend that you make a logical progression with your social engineering testing. For many of my clients it is the first time they have undertaken serious social engineering testing and this progression makes sense for them. You may have engaged a traditional penetration testing company that offers elements of social engineering. However, this is rarely done in a systematic way that can lead to an effective development programme. Rather, it often just exploits one or two obvious holes and then demonstrates the extent to which they can be breached.

A better approach is to think in terms of three levels of progression.

Levels of Progression

LEVEL ONE – NO INSIDE INFORMATION

I wouldn't call this 'zero knowledge' as I would be gathering information from the first time I enter the organization for a planning meeting (or even prior to that, just engaging with them on the telephone). However, my level of knowledge would be restricted to publicly available information or the information that any casual visitor could pick up.

I would usually recommend this approach as a good starting point for a first engagement with a new client unless they have had extensive testing already that has addressed this need.

This is a good simulation of an attack conducted by someone without any specific insider knowledge and therefore matches the type of attack for a large number of threat scenarios. However, accepted wisdom within information security tells us that the insider threat may be as much as 80 per cent of the threat; with attackers either coming from the inside or having insider help in their attack.

Therefore you may well want to move to levels two and three quite quickly.

LEVEL TWO – INSIDER INFORMATION

At this level I utilize specific insider information. This is often a combination of information we may have gleaned from level one testing, combined with particular information supplied by the client. The exact nature of the information supplied is selected to relate to the various information or system targets chosen for the testing.

I would normally recommend that you analyse the results of level one testing and select areas that either were not covered adequately or perhaps target the testing of some of the new protective countermeasures that have been introduced since the first initial testing.

When measurement of security improvements is done well it can offer great benefits. This is particularly the case when demonstrating effectiveness to senior managers (the ones who have usually made the decision to invest).

LEVEL THREE TESTING – ACTIVE INSIDER HELP

To add a new level of realism to the testing, as we progress to this third level we get an employee (this may be you?) to join the testing team. This person not only supplies inside information, they also take an active role in assisting the attack.

My reasons for using an existing employee to act as the insider is often partly to keep the costs down. The alternative is for one of the testing team to take a long-term assignment by getting a job in the target organization. This is not good use of consulting time when you usually have a ready supply of existing employees.

Now you may think that this would make a social engineering testing job too easy. For example, rather than working out ways to trick entry into the building, the employee simply signs the tester in. However, you must remember that testing will already have covered all these types of attack at levels one and two. Also, if you think that a social engineering attack with insider involvement is just too easy, then I hope that your risk assessment includes this and you have invested in some really effective staff vetting and monitoring.

Social Engineering Testing Methodology

At ECSC, I have often used the following methodology for testing an organization's social engineering vulnerabilities. This is usually an approach I would use for a level one – 'no inside information' testing programme.

Whilst the exact details are matched to specific requirements, the following outline will show you some common elements:

STAGE ONE – PUBLIC INFORMATION GATHERING

You may be surprised how much of your information is already in the public domain. This may come from your suppliers or partners, quite regularly on their websites. Another useful source is the variety of Internet postings your employees make, leaking information that, when collated, can be very interesting to an attacker. I often find technical staff making postings, and asking questions online, that give out very valuable information regarding your systems – often specifically related to security countermeasures. On occasion these postings have included descriptions of current problems with security countermeasures. Recent entries such as 'we are still having problems with our intrusion detection system' are especially interesting to a hacker.

For social engineering testing purposes, we are interested in as much detail about the potential target's information and systems as possible.

STAGE TWO – PEOPLE INFORMATION GATHERING

Further investigation then begins to uncover useful information about your employees. Temporary employment availability and information about employee activities outside of the workplace can all be useful.

Building up a database of employees, roles and interesting information is an important element in the preparation for an attack.

STAGE THREE – TARGET SELECTION

Depending upon their role and/or observed behaviour, certain people will be chosen. Following initial contact, targets can be profiled according to their usefulness to an attacker. During this process, relationship building is occurring that makes any final exploitation so much easier.

Once we identify specific employees, usually selected because of their role, we can often find out lots of interesting personal information that can help us conduct an attack. Social networking sites can be particularly useful for this. Instant rapport is much more likely when a target finds out that we share the same hobby (even though I only adopted it 15 seconds before I made the call!).

STAGE FOUR – TARGET EXPLOITATION

At this stage we could begin to bring in some elements of technology, depending upon the specification agreed with the client. A number of attack scenarios can be tested, combining human, technical and physical security.

For 'pure' social engineering testing we will either be conducting remote testing or gaining entry and interacting with the business as part of the test.

STAGE FIVE – REPORTING

A risk analysis usually forms the basis of a full report to help you address your vulnerabilities. We also compare our tests with any alerts generated by the more aware employees.

Reporting is often at a number of levels and may include the development of presentations in addition to the usual written report. It is important that appropriate formats are used for particular groups.

A typical written test report may include:

Executive summary

In any form of consulting it is important to capture the essential elements in bite-sized chunks for senior managers. Drawing pictures and graphs can help too.

Only yesterday I was feeding back a social engineering testing exercise to a client in a 1 hour 30 minute session. However, something told me that the CTO would not give us that much time so I asked him how long I should take. He then announced that he had another meeting booked in 20 minutes! Without my prompting he would probably have just made his apologies at that point and left. However, after obtaining the critical information, I was able to take the highlights from each section in the 20-page report. In this case I didn't use the Executive Summary page itself, however, I covered each of the main points it outlined throughout the report (especially using the various diagrams and graphs). Timing my finish with 2 minutes to go, I simply had enough time to ask him if there was any other information he needed. When he said he just wanted costs for doing the next stage, I was able to point him to the last page, where we had mapped out the next 9 months of development. He left happy.

Headline risks identified

Although mentioned in the Executive Summary, I like to outline each of the headline risks identified in testing, prioritizing their risk level for the client. This may not be a fully ISO 27001 compliant risk assessment, however it gives the client the benefit of our experience and in effect an action plan of improvements.

Testing specification, scope and limitations

You never test everything and therefore the risks uncovered can rarely be comprehensive. It is important to clearly define the areas covered by the testing, its scope and limitations. I prefer to mention the various elements and approaches not included in the test to illustrate the point. This is much better than just stating that the test is limited as it gives the reader a much better understanding. In addition, it helps the client think about the next stage in their testing programme.

Testing methodologies deployed

In addition to the overall specification and exclusions, a report should clearly explain the testing methodologies used. Nothing should be hidden as this doesn't help you to understand your vulnerabilities.

Whilst not going into the detail contained within these pages, a report should help you understand the range of tests and why they are relevant.

Test results (including client generated alarms)

I strongly recommend that you document every test, rather than just the ones that worked. On occasion I get to see other people's social engineering test reports (when the client asks me for my opinion). I often find they just outline one attack (the one that worked) and then go to great lengths to show what they could do to exploit the social engineering weaknesses. These usually just exploit one obvious hole in the client's defences and in many cases the client was well aware of the vulnerability. In effect they offer little value, unless they can be used to get the attention of other senior managers.

Better to document all the tests to give the client a good overall picture of their strengths and weaknesses.

Another valuable area to explore is to compare the various tests with any alerts generated within the organization. It is worth thinking about how good your detection mechanisms are at detecting potential social engineering attacks.

TRY TO GET CAUGHT

Yes, that is correct. An effective tester should try to get caught. Simply demonstrating immense social engineering skills to defeat all your defences doesn't allow you to measure your security level.

Ideally a testing project should have a mixture of:

- failed tests that were identified by the client and thwarted;

- tests that worked, yet did generate an alert at some point after;

- tests that worked and were undetected.

This allows you to clearly see the effective level of your security. If all tests either fail or succeed then you don't actually know how good your security is.

It is important that testing doesn't become more of a measure of the testers' skill than a test of your security.

The above isn't necessarily very easy, as a failed test may generate so much 'noise' within your organization that further testing is then too easily identified by expectant staff who are all very consciously looking for attacks. However, you can manage this situation by having a professional way to deal with employees who do successfully detect an attack. We call this our 'get of jail free card'.

Get Out of Jail Free Cards

A good con artist will always have a convincing excuse for their behaviour and a justification for their actions designed to 'get them off the hook'. A trick that can be deployed during a social engineering attack is also known as a 'get out of jail free card'. We use such a device during our social engineering testing exercises.

Given that we don't want a testing exercise 'spoilt' by alarms from a suspicious target alerting other employees to our attacks, we carry a letter from the chief executive, or similar high ranking manager/officer, along the following lines:

[Company letterhead]

Dear employee

THIS IS A SECURITY TEST

If you have been shown this letter, then I must personally congratulate you on being vigilant and aware. [Company name] needs more people with your attention to detail to protect our assets and keep our people secure.

We have employed ECSC to test our security. You will understand that to make this a true test we could not warn you. The person showing you this letter will make a note of your details and your successful detection of the test will be reported to the management team in their final report.

I ask you to keep the details of this test to yourself, as even your line manager will not be aware of this exercise. Your support in our efforts to enhance our security is greatly appreciated.

Yours faithfully

[Executive signature]
[Executive name]

Now this may sound quite reasonable in a testing situation. However, the letter is not genuine. We construct this ourselves with no involvement from the management of the commissioning organization. The letterhead is easily obtained as most organizations send many out each day. The signature is easily scanned from the annual accounts.

We do have a genuine letter, actually signed from a senior manager.

[Company letterhead]

Dear employee

THIS IS A SECURITY TEST

We have employed ECSC to test our security. You will understand that to make this a true test we could not warn you. The person showing you this letter will make a note of your details and your successful detection of the test will be reported to the management team in their final report.

The tests have been planned for the week beginning Monday [Date]

It is important that you verify this letter be contacting someone on the following list, each of whom are aware of these tests. Please use the internal telephone directory to contact them.

Person one

Person two

Person three

The following personnel from ECSC are conducting the test and will be able to show you photographic ID to verify their identity:

Consultant one

Consultant two

Consultant three

I ask you to keep the details of this test to yourself for the remainder of this week as even your line manager may not be aware of this exercise. Your support in our efforts to enhance our security is greatly appreciated.

Yours faithfully

[Executive signature]
[Executive name]

PS If the consultants tried to trick you with the fake letter first, then extra congratulations on your vigilance.

In our experience, most people who do detect an attack can be persuaded by the first letter. However, they did successfully identify an attack was being conducted. A small amount of guidance and training is all that is necessary to give them a better way to confirm a test and report an incident.

Another variation on this technique was used by a group of students at my local university.

I help out with two Masters courses at the university in computer security and computer forensics. In return for my time delivering some lectures, the course tutors point us in the direction of the most talented students. We then recruit the best. Everyone wins.

One of the exercises I recently conducted had the following brief:

SESSION ONE – SOCIAL ENGINEERING INTRODUCTION

In this session you will be introduced to some of the common elements in a social engineering attack. In addition you will learn some of the advanced psychology used by attackers to achieve their aims. The session will also introduce you to some elements of the ECSC Social Engineering Testing Methodology.

EXERCISE ONE – SOCIAL ENGINEERING TESTING

You are to plan an attack on the University. Before you read any further, stop. Examine the section below on professional conduct and think about how this relates to this exercise.

You will be working in groups of three or four.

TASK ONE – VULNERABILITY IDENTIFICATION

Identify a vulnerability, or vulnerabilities, in the University's information security that could be exploited using social engineering techniques. Document this weakness, together with the potential consequences if this vulnerability were to be exploited. Typical outcomes could be sight or removal of documents, electronic access to systems or physical access to an area.

TASK TWO – EXPLOIT PLANNING

Plan precisely how your team could exploit the vulnerability identified in Task One. This exploitation must target the weakness and be clear in the techniques you would use. Be precise in the identification of your objective. Also, try to identify key risk points for the attacker and how these could be minimized to avoid getting caught.

Create a succinct report or presentation covering the two tasks. Please bring three copies of this to Session Two.

WARNING: THERE IS NO TASK THREE

You are not to conduct the planned attack or share the plan outside of the course. Not everyone in the University hierarchy is as understanding and open minded as your course tutors. You must leave this fun for your possible future career as a consultant.

SESSION TWO – SOCIAL ENGINEERING FEEDBACK

In this session, you will have the opportunity to share and discuss Exercise One.

PROFESSIONAL CONDUCT AND CONFIDENTIALITY

There may be elements in the above sessions and exercises where you may uncover vulnerabilities in the university's systems. You will notice that at no point in any session will Ian Mann have named, or given 'clues' as to the identity of, ECSC's clients. However, other contributors may not have been so careful. Assuming you want a career in information security, then it is important that you now begin to follow the highest levels of professional conduct, both during and following these sessions. This is particularly important in relation to Exercise One. You are expected to maintain confidentiality at all times. Think before you discuss vulnerabilities in public, be careful where you store or transmit electronic information and take care when printing and disposing of documents.

Anyway, back to the use of 'get out of jail free cards'. In a recent example of the above exercise, a group of particularly able students hatched a very complex and elaborate plan to dress up as contractors doing some electrical work and use this cover to plant network sniffers at strategic points on the network. I kindly didn't mention that their student access probably gave them all the access they would need as they had obviously spent a good few hours on the exercise, planning every detail even down to the cost of acquiring the appropriate work clothes.

Their 'get out of jail free card' was a fake work order for doing electrical work for the university. However, they missed a trick. Their planned work order was open to challenge. If caught, always a possibility in face-to-face social engineering attacks, the person challenging them may have some in-depth knowledge of the actual contractors used. A better strategy than a correct work order is to construct a wrong work order!

Let me explain. Imagine if, when challenged, rather than producing a work order for the university, they produce one for the local college. This is conveniently on a site adjoining the university's. This gives an extremely elegant, 'Oh, isn't this the college?' excuse for the work in progress and a reason to exit without undue suspicion.

Targeted Testing

'Capture the Flag'-type attacks can be great fun and, on occasions, present some interesting challenges. Examples of this include:

- get into your data centre or server room;

- obtain information from the CEO's office (PLEASE get their approval first);

- get a sample of your confidential designs.

This can be as targeted as obtaining a copy of a specific named document.

The key feature of this type of testing that can, depending upon your protection strength, be a particular challenge is that:

- You often cannot afford to fail. In most test situations the tester can be detected and simply move on to other targets. Alternatively, the tester can 'back off' before they are detected and then target other easier employees. With a very targeted scope, you may not have this option.

- With only a single attack vector, the tester may have some very strong people to bypass. In most social engineering scenarios an attacker has a wide choice of attacks. By definition, an attacker will be choosing the attack that they think will be the easiest. With too targeted a test, you may just be asking the tester to attack the strongest element of your security. This may not help you uncover new vulnerabilities.

MAKING IT REALLY DIFFICULT

If you want to be really tough on your testers, give them a really targeted attack and tell the potential targets that the attack is imminent. In my experience, this is the most challenging scenario, however, also the most satisfying when accomplished successfully in a short space of time.

The Power of the Cardboard Box – A Typical Testing Assignment

At the time of writing this final chapter, I am sat at my desk in a hotel in the City of London – the heart of the financial district. We are currently halfway through a social engineering test for a client. Clearly I won't be giving any details that could distinguish them from the hundreds of other financial organizations within this area. However, some of the approaches, challenges and interesting findings make it worth sharing with you.

The testing assignment is relatively short, 2 people for 3 days; 1 day preparation, 1 day testing and 1 day reporting.

Having actually started the testing last night, continuing with more early this morning and planning to return this evening, I am taking a break to write this account.

However, before sharing with you some of the details, I will map out the scope of the assignment.

TESTING SCOPE

In common with many initial social engineering tests, we have not had much information to work with. A previous meeting with the client was confined to a quick briefing to outline the requirements.

The scope is quite simple:

- gain physical entry to the building;

- interact internally, including copying documents;

- conduct a simple network/systems vulnerability scan.

This brief was supplemented with some potential target information:

1. staff salary and bonus information;

2. senior management information;

3. client reports;

4. employee or client personal information.

Along with this brief were some agreed areas that were to be out of scope, including:

- no advanced contact and associated relationship building – this is to be left for subsequent testing;

- no removal of documents or property, as this would likely lead to some business disruption;

- no bugging or covert camera installation;

- no remote testing;

- no destructive elements within the vulnerability scan.

PREPARATION

The inclusion of the technical vulnerability scan of the network and critical internal systems means that I have to be accompanied by one of our technical consultants. Although not very experienced in social engineering, he is very keen and highly competent and experienced at conducting technical testing.

WEAKNESS IDENTIFICATION

From the initial meeting, I picked up a weakness in the reception. As is common with most swipe barrier entry systems, there is a method to bypass the barriers. Waiting in reception, I noticed a number of people entering reception from another internal door, avoiding the barriers. In addition, the receptionists opened this door for someone entering the building.

Clearly this gives an opportunity to trick the receptionists into giving us access. With employees running into the hundreds, it is very unlikely that the receptionist will recognize everyone.

As a visitor, I was only given a simple identification badge (no picture) and no swipe access – another reason why the extra door from reception to the inside is necessary.

I took the opportunity to photograph my visitor badge with my mobile phone (during a comfort break) at the planning meeting. This was a precaution if I was forced to hand it in. However, I managed to retain this as I left so the photograph was not needed.

Preparation included copying the badges and creating them for my colleague and myself for the 3 days of testing. In addition, we requested the official letter previously discussed from the client and subsequently used it as a template to create the fake letter.

We also obtained a couple of large cardboard boxes – more of that later.

Our standard attack kit contains a number of keyboard logging devices, cameras of various sizes, other useful items (like clipboards) to adopt different roles and a wireless access point.

Although remote testing is out of scope, we have done some Internet-based research, both on the client website and also through search engines. This allowed us to identify all the senior executives, along with some employment history and a host of other employee information including a group within a social networking site dedicated to current and past employees. This has already come in useful to clarify certain people we have targeted and also to give us names to drop in terms of who we are working with.

Clearly, at the preparation stage, we had very little information about internal weaknesses so we needed to do some initial on-site surveillance.

ATTACK ONE

I thought a straightforward bypass of the reception entry barriers was a good place to start, so last night as employees began to leave, we entered.

We wanted to give the impression that we were already visitors who had just popped out for a coffee (I only buy coffee when doing social engineering attacks!).

Armed with our fake badges we entered the reception. We carried no bags or coats as these would have been left inside if we had simply left to get a coffee.

I 'instructed' the receptionist to let us in, saying we had just gone out for a drink. The receptionist gave a weak challenge to ask us who we were with, so we showed the badges and named the manager we had selected. She then proceeded to let us in. Simple.

We then proceeded to take the lift to all floors to map out the various departments. Helpfully, the client placed department names at key locations so this didn't take too long. We found some internal swipe access, however nothing that would hinder our progress.

We found some key locations for use further into the attack:

- the client meeting rooms;

- an open communications room high up, and adjacent to an exterior wall, perfect for a wireless installation;

- the executive suite.

In the process of this initial visit, we took some opportunities to do a little more:

- On finding the executive suite relatively empty, we attached a keyboard sniffer to a PC within an office for one of our key targets. This would give us the opportunity to do a simple retrieval 24 hours later.

- We also photographed the full meeting itinerary for the following day (helpfully left at the reception for the meeting rooms floor). We suspected that the schedule would be full and wanted to find some gaps for our own use the following day.

As we suspected, examination of the copied meeting schedule showed that the meeting floor was going to be very busy the next day. An early start would be necessary.

ATTACK TWO

Having already tested the receptionist, we decided this morning to test the overnight security guards. Someone has already (helpfully) told us the times when receptionists hand over to the security guards, and vice versa.

This is where the cardboard boxes came in handy. I decided that we would adopt the role of employees bringing in some boxes of materials for an important meeting in the boardroom. The boxes serve a couple of purposes, as they would:

- allow us to hide a number of items within them;
- make traversing the barriers (that happen to be full height) very difficult.

So our gaining entry, past the reception manned by security guards, was made possible by pretending to be employees.

Unfortunately, the guards spoilt this by asking to see our IDs (which we clearly didn't have). I suspected as much as we approached. Based on the previous night's surveillance visit, I had hoped for a single guard. On seeing two, I knew the chances of them complying strictly with their process was increased. (People are often easier to trick into cutting corners with process when they are not with colleagues.)

A quick switch to plan B was needed. I pulled out my (fake) visitor badge and told him we were meeting someone and had already been there for a couple of days.

Then quite a strange thing happened. The guard took the fake badge, took it out of the holder and proceeded to interrogate the visitor IT system. I assumed the game was up and prepared to show them the letter(s) regarding the test. However, I have been doing this long enough to know not to jump in too quickly, so I waited. I then observed the guard who proceeded to recreate a new genuine badge for me and then ask for the details of my colleague so he could do the same for him. Then the other guard proceeded to show us up to the boardroom where he left us to get on with our task.

Unexpected to say the least. However, in social engineering testing the unexpected is often to be expected! At the moment, I can only assume the guard mistakenly thought the badge I gave him was for the previous day, and then followed his normal pattern of issuing visitor badges.

Once we gained access, my colleague proceeded to the target area for wireless installation. He installed the access point so it could not be easily discovered, quickly tested it from a hand-held device and photographed the installation.

I proceeded to a meeting room where the previous evening I noticed a laptop with a memory stick attached. As the scope excludes the removal of property, I couldn't take the laptop, however I did take a copy of the memory stick contents. This included a number of internal presentations by different people, including some elements of concern from a confidentiality perspective.

Using our previously obtained meeting itinerary, we found a meeting room that we could gain network access from. My colleague proceeded to complete the network scan. This showed that the meeting areas were not segregated at a network level and he quickly gained full access to the domain.

Whilst he did this, I decided to check on the keyboard sniffer added the previous night. With only limited testing time, I was concerned that the target manager might not be in and our efforts could be wasted. Given that his office is 'guarded' by the executive PAs, I needed a reason for entry. I decided to combine this with obtaining some further usernames and passwords.

I decided to do some further keyboard logging to get passwords.

The executive PAs were quite pleased when this pleasant gentleman turned up to survey the speed of their PCs. The implication being that perhaps new ones would be arriving soon. I asked if anyone was complaining about the speed. When asked if new PCs were coming soon, I replied that I assumed so given the age of these and that I presumed executives were being given some priority.

My surveying of computer speed was quite simple:

- the user logs out;
- I check the details of the machine. This needed me to go on my hands and knees under the desk, giving a perfect opportunity to install the logger;

- as the user logged in, I timed the event, commenting that it was either quite fast or quite slow. Either gave me the excuse to double check the PC for performance and retrieve the logger.

As it turned out, it was good to go back as the original target was not in work today and our efforts would have been wasted. So I turned my attention to the PAs.

They were very helpful, indicating that they could test not only their own PCs, but also their colleagues. Unfortunately, when one PA tried the password it didn't work. She solved this by examining a post-it note from her colleague's desk drawer! That will be worth photographing tonight to see if any other logins are recorded.

My subsequent discussion with the PAs also revealed that they both work for the chairman, who doesn't use a PC. Therefore, it is likely we now have access to all his confidential information.

We then both left the building, again keeping our visitor badges for a subsequent attack later in the day.

ATTACK THREE

We entered the building again towards the end of the normal working day (although given the nature of the organization, we expected quite a few employees to be there for a few hours more).

Firstly I took my colleague back to the meeting rooms, so he could conduct some further network investigations. By now, I had a good rapport with the young lady on the meeting floor reception and she helpfully found us a room that would be free for the rest of the evening. Even though she only met us within the last 24 hours and has not authenticated our identity in any way, she now treats us as friends.

I took the opportunity to visit the Human Resources (HR) department before everyone left. I wanted to do a repeat of the computer speed test. In addition, I wanted access to the key HR applications that would give access to salary and bonus information.

As it turned out, the whole department were still at their desks and were more than happy to help in my testing. The manager did ask who I was working for, however, when given the name of the head of IT, she accepted that and then was most helpful.

The adding of keyboard loggers underneath desks in the dark is a bit tricky and I did joke with them that I could do with a torch 'to identify the model on these computers'.

Armed with a key-logger with multiple user credentials, together with notes detailing the usernames that were cached, I returned for analysis and to try the logins remotely.

Having successfully obtained access to the target key information, I decided a further 'walk through' of the whole office would be an interesting exercise. By now many staff had left, however, there were still enough people present to give us an opportunity to test their general awareness. We still wanted to identify what would alert people to our presence.

Therefore, we began to move around the offices taking photos. This was not done covertly; my colleague had a standard 'compact' zoom camera and I was armed with a full-size SLR camera with sizeable zoom lens (great for document photography!).

We headed for the senior management suite first to see what documents we could find. We also wanted to photograph the post-it note with passwords. To the credit of the PA, she had locked the drawer with this in.

We then proceeded to HR (expecting the office to be locked), to find the door wide open and everyone gone home. Not only did we get many document copies, but we could also access cabinets full of payroll data – a bonus as this was a target.

Further movement through the offices found post-it notes with logins and passwords (passwords are bad enough, however to be given the login is just making life too easy).

There was too much information to copy, so we focused on showing desks with confidential documents, laptops left in the open and printers full of uncollected printouts.

To make our activities a little more noticeable, I also turned on the powerful flash on my camera to complement its loud click every time I took a photo.

Despite my best efforts, I didn't get a single challenge. Perhaps my instruction to my colleague to 'look like a photographer's assistant' worked a treat.

CONCLUSION

We hit all our target information. The client was particularly impressed with gaining access to the chairman's email (through his PA).

Given that this was the first social engineering test, and given the level of access we achieved, we made a point of not actually viewing information. We had photographic evidence and passwords for key users that would give us easy access to the target information. In addition, with over 6 hours of time within their offices, we had plenty of opportunity to use it.

In our experience, you need to prove what can be done. However, going over the top with accessing confidential information can just annoy senior managers without demonstrating more risk. Our intention is to help improve security, not humiliate individuals or 'rub it in' when people have weak systems.

CLIENT ALERTS

Within this test, the client did uncover some activities. This is good. As previously discussed, 100 per cent 'success' doesn't tell you how good your security is; it only tells you how 'great' we are at testing.

I have deliberately left out some instances of where we were discovered, however, these fall into three broad categories:

1. A challenge dealt with through a believable response, not indicating the test is in progress.

2. People who accept the fake letter, or equivalent.

Individuals who need the genuine letter and do the appropriate follow-up checks.

In addition, we sometimes find that people can raise an alarm at a later stage and this is useful to ascertain within the reporting stage.

By leaving out these details, combined with the subsequent improvements planned by the client, I am satisfied that even if you recognized them, you wouldn't be able to use any of the above account to help you attack them.

Developing Stronger Systems

Although the focus of this last chapter is on the testing of social engineering, these activities should also help you to develop even stronger systems. Therefore, I wanted to share with you some ideas about the development of protection to new levels that can better withstand social engineering attack.

In my experience, there are two pathways towards the development of even stronger systems:

PATHWAY ONE – REMOVE PEOPLE FROM THE SYSTEM ALTOGETHER

If we agree that people are usually the weakest link, then removing them should be a worthwhile aspiration. If users do not have access to the most critical information, then an attacker cannot trick them into sending them the information.

This way of thinking goes against the grain of many developments in information, communications and technologies, where connecting systems and sharing information is often the goal. By contrasting these goals with sound information security thinking, we can achieve the goals of greater information availability with appropriate security where it is needed most.

Let's use a very simple example to illustrate the point:

I was recently involved in an analysis of credit card information for a client seeking to develop their Payment Card Industry (PCI) Data Security Standard (DSS) compliance. We were looking at a particularly open system, where credit card data was stored within a database without encryption, and including items such as the three-digit security code on the rear of the card. Both of these 'features' are in breach of the DSS.

Having identified this weak system, we began to explore who had access. On investigation, it was revealed that each user of the database actually had full administration rights to all the data. This was 'necessary' for some functionality. However, for 'necessary' read 'unnecessary', as this was just a shortcut to save time and effort in correctly implementing a system with appropriate security and functionality.

In its current state, any of the 250+ users can simply take a copy of all the credit card data. With over 50 000 credit card details, at the going rate on the underground market of $20 per card, I can think of about a million reasons why someone may be tempted to steal this data.

By restricting access to single records, and developing simple alerts for users going over and above a 'normal' rate of accessing records, we did two things:

1. Reduced the potential attackers from 250+ down to just a few administrators.

2. Introduced a detection mechanism to highlight suspicious behaviour from the users with necessary access to the data.

This work was carried out whilst simultaneously encrypting the card data and removing the unnecessary security codes from the database.

We have therefore gone from open information with multiple users, to encrypted data with very few people with access to all the information. An easy social engineering target, with easy insider access, now becomes relatively difficult. Certainly, a would-be attacker could now find an easier target elsewhere.

PATHWAY TWO – GET PEOPLE TO PROCESS AT A CONSCIOUS LEVEL

I see many occasions where people are in key roles within an information security system and they are clearly operating 'on autopilot', making them easy targets for social engineering manipulation. Much of my analysis for the human component in security is to get people to have to think more consciously, and therefore more likely to identify and thwart a potential attack.

It is clear that testing can play a big role in this, raising awareness and getting people to question events that otherwise would have gone undetected. However, we can redesign work flows to avoid people getting into this position.

Where I see bank call centre operators doing their job, and simultaneously managing their online auctions, I know that they are open to social engineering manipulation. Where the emphasis has been on 'efficiency' and simplifying roles for mass operation, the operation can quickly drop into subconscious activity where persuasion becomes quite easy for the skilled social engineer.

In the current environment of rich pickings for the social engineer, you do not have to go too far in your countermeasure development to make your organization a poor target. There are still a number of organizations doing nothing, and you can let them become the next target.

My work to date convinces me that social engineering attacks are being hugely successful without currently having to be very sophisticated. Many of the psychological techniques covered in this book are beyond the understanding, and usual armoury, of a typical attacker. However, be warned, they are learning fast.

If security can be broken with the very simplest of techniques, we will need to pay much more attention to effective countermeasures as the attackers develop more advanced techniques. The incentive, measured by monetary gain, is there.

Final Thoughts

In my experience, many information systems are now developed from the underlying assumption that sharing the maximum amount of information is good; security is often a necessary afterthought. In addition, most organizations are designed on the assumption 'that it will not happen to us', playing down the external threat and ignoring the insider attacks. The constant stream of high-profile breaches, and considerably more that never get any publicity, are starting to focus people on security.

In writing this book, I have had the opportunity to share with you a range of experiences, discoveries, thoughts and theories in the area of social engineering.

Given the relative infancy of the discipline of social engineering understanding, development and testing, I consider this book to be just the start. One of the challenges I face is constantly wanting to update each section with new ideas and reflecting our experiences in solving client problems. However, at the time of writing this, I am 2 weeks away from a self-imposed deadline, when I hand over a manuscript to the publisher and start to catch up on the other exciting developments that have been put on hold for these final few weeks.

Whilst having to fit this around developing an information security services organization, and doing my fair share of consultancy work, I still hope you share my view that it has been worthwhile. You may not agree with everything in these pages and I hope that some areas have challenged your beliefs regarding human behaviour and thinking. However, it is my intention that your personal understanding has developed. I trust you will have found something that can help you solve your personal information security challenges to the benefit of your organization and the wider community.

Looking forward, I eagerly await further developments in this area. As more information security professionals begin to lift the lid on social engineering as a new discipline, we shall find the sharing of ideas begins to catch up with the criminal enterprises that have long since discovered social engineering's value to them. It is my firm belief that we can redress the balance and create an exciting technological environment with its multitude of benefits, yet combine this with security to allow us to exploit its full potential.

In trying to fill a gap in the mass of current IT security publications, I have added my input to redressing some balance in information security thinking towards the human element. We still have a long way to go. Some of the methodologies I have developed can still be refined, extended and adapted to offer new insight into human vulnerabilities and associated protection development.

I consider myself very fortunate in being able to help such a diverse range of clients and having the privilege of working with such a talented team at ECSC. From my fellow consultants, to my technical engineers, sales consultants and our support team, they are the most committed individuals I have ever had the pleasure of working with. They, along with our clients, deserve my thanks for making my job such a rewarding challenge.

Thank you to Jonathan Norman at Gower Publishing for proposing the book, his constructive feedback throughout, and especially his patience. Also, thanks to Jenny Hallas for help in the psychology elements, and a special thanks to Lucy Allison at ECSC for many late nights reading my numerous drafts, and suggesting so many improvements.

And finally, I thank you for purchasing this book, and getting to the final page. Feel free to drop me a line with your thoughts and experiences in the field of social engineering, and I hope we get the chance to meet at some point.

Further Reading

Rather than a dry academic set of references, I thought you would appreciate a quick guided tour of the highlights of my library, related to social engineering. Below you will find a delightful mixture of easy reading, combined with some in-depth analytical texts. Some new and some a little older.

As a general principle, I find most mainstream academic psychology to be detached from my clients' expectations in solving real information security problems – they need rapid results from clear, understandable frameworks that can be re-applied. However, the easy reading-type approach often lacks the intellectual rigour to move beyond simple observations and untested theory.

In my experience, the best results can be found by tracking back to the originators of ideas and theories, examining their first works on the area. Therefore, I tend to bypass the plethora of later works that expand, twist and distort the original gems. This is particularly applicable to areas such as NLP, where the early work of Bandler and Grinder has so much more to offer than the numerous recent books and masses of training courses.

So I have mapped a course through a selection of texts. Feel free to dip into areas of interest, reject any that don't work for you, and send me details of additional works that you think I would like.

Neuro-Linguistic Programming (NLP)

Patterns of the Hypnotic Techniques of Milton E. Erickson
Richard Bandler and John Grinder
(Meta Publications, 1975, ISBN 978-1555520526)

Patterns of the Hypnotic Techniques of Milton E. Erickson Vol II
John Grinder, Judith Delozier and Richard Bandler
(Meta Publications, 1977, ISBN 1-55552-053-7)

Although academic in tone, these are the original texts that led to the development of NLP. As with the two below, none of the later over-hyped and almost religious approach to personal development; just real insight into the human mind.

The Structure of Magic I
Richard Bandler and John Grinder
(Science and Behavior Books, 1975, ISBN 08314-0044-7)

What better recommendation than from Erickson himself, who said, 'I learned a great deal about the things that I've done without knowing about them.'

The Structure of Magic II
Richard Bandler and John Grinder
(Science and Behavior Books, 1976, ISBN 08314-0049-8)

Don't be put off by the formal notation developed in the above texts; it really is a useful framework for the analysis of thinking. You can also trace this to later work by people such as Anthony Robbins. I thought Robbins worth a mention, I left out his work deliberately as it is more useful for personal development than analysis of social engineering. However, his books should be on your bookshelf.

Magic in Action
Richard Bandler
(Meta Publications, 1992, ISBN 0-916990-14-1)

Time for a Change
Richard Bandler
(Meta Publications, 1993, ISBN 0-916990-28-1)

I put these two in as interesting examples of where Bandler moved the original theories in NLP as a distinct set of principles. You may feel that some of the later works are more to support the growing NLP industry of training courses. However, you will still find more value in Bandler's contributions than the thousands of spin-offs. I always find it slightly amusing when people who 'master' NLP then only apply it to teaching other people more NLP. Much better to take the early principles and apply them to other fields – such as information security!

Risk

The Book of Risk
Dan Borge
(Wiley, 2001, ISBN 978-0471323785)

The quote on the back cover sums up my view of this accessible little book: 'Failure to read and to heed Borge on risk is an unacceptable risk.' Although, in places, the focus on explaining financial risk may put some people off, overall this is a great place to start if you want to learn more. It is worth remembering that with many of the people selling you financial products today, using some of the persuasion skills discussed in this book, there has never been a better time to understand the financial side of risk.

Hypnotherapy

If you find the early NLP work as fascinating as I do, then you may want to expand your reading into further study of Erickson. The two texts below are a great starting point. Some people could find the focus on helping dysfunctional individuals a little strange for study into developing information security countermeasures, however it all depends upon how dysfunctional you think the average employee may be.

My Voice Will Go With You – The Teaching Tales of Milton H. Erickson
Sidney Rosen
(Norton, 1991, ISBN 0-393-30135-4)

Uncommon Therapy – The Psychiatric Techniques of Milton H. Erickson
Jay Haley
(Norton, 1993, ISBN 0-393-31031-0)

Worth having on your shelves as a fascinating set of experiments that give a glimpse as to the power of the subconscious; you should find yourself a copy of the following:

Time Distortion in Hypnosis – An Experimental and Clinical Investigation
Linn F. Cooper and Milton H. Erickson
(Crown House, 2002, ISBN 1-89983-695-0) Originally published in 1959.

Hypnosis

If the above strikes up an interest in hypnosis, or you simply want to bypass the therapy side of things, then the following are a great introduction to the various strands of hypnosis.

Monsters and Magical Sticks – There's No Such Thing as Hypnosis
Steven Heller and Terry Steele
(New Falcon, 1987, ISBN 1-56184-026-2)

If you only ever read one book on hypnosis, then this should be it. Although, I guarantee that having read it you will want to read more. It is a wonderfully engaging text that clearly puts hypnosis in the context of our everyday thinking.

Having read the above, you could then be interested in how hypnosis has been used to develop the stage acts that many people see as its only application. For a clear and easy explanation of stage techniques, you should look to:

Deeper and Deeper – Secrets of Stage Hypnosis
Jonathan Chase
(Academy of Hypnotic Arts, 2005, ISBN 0-9547098-1-0)

Whilst not trying too hard to explain the process of hypnosis in any depth, the clear description of the techniques that work will give you a great insight into this area.

If you prefer to explore self-hypnosis, and want to explore your own subconscious then I can recommend:

The Secrets of Self-Hypnosis
Adam Eason
(Network 3000 Publishing, 2005, ISBN 0-9709321-9-7)

A great source of simple techniques that can be used for all varieties of self-help processes. You really can get in touch with the real you!

Hypnotic Suggestion

These are a selection of NLP and hypnosis-related texts on suggestion and use of language. Whilst not quite as interesting as the above, they do help to relate some of the above theory into social engineering techniques.

Words that Change Minds – Mastering the Language of Influence
Shelle Rose Charvet
(Kendall/Hunt, 1995, ISBN 0-7872-3479-6)

Sleight of Mouth – The Magic of Conversational Belief Change
Robert Dilts
(Meta Publications, 1999, ISBN 0-916990-43-5)

Wordweaving – The Science of Suggestion
Trevor Silvester
(The Quest Institute, 2003, ISBN 0-9543664-0-9)

Transactional Analysis

As with NLP, I think you will gain more from these original texts than the many more recent and less interesting reworkings. At various times through writing this book I considered completely removing TA. However, I now believe my reticence was more to do with needing to explore the area in more depth and produce more working frameworks for client problems. I would be interested in your thoughts.

Games People Play – The Psychology of Human Relationships
Eric Berne
(Penguin Books, 1964, ISBN 0-14-002768-8)

What Do You Say After You Say Hello?
Eric Berne
(Corgi, 1975, ISBN 0-552-09806-X)

I'm Okay You're Okay
Thomas A. Harris
(Arrow, 1995, ISBN 0-09-955241-8) First published as 'The Book of Choice' in 1970.

Staying Okay
Amy and Thomas Harris
(Arrow, 1995, ISBN 0-09-955251-5) First published in 1985.

Psychic Powers

If you ever need a new and interesting income stream from your 'natural psychic ability' then this is a great place to start. Alternatively, if you just want to understand how easy it is to manipulate people into believing, then this is the book for you.

The Full Facts Book of Cold Reading
Ian Rowland
(Ian Rowland, 1998) Available direct from Ian's website www.ianrowland.com

Body Language

There really is too much written on this subject and too many people who think that simply copying how someone is sitting will instantly get them to follow your every command. However, if you do want to learn more then this is the most authoritative work.

People Watching
Desmond Morris
(Vintage, 2002, ISBN 0-099-42978-0) (update version of the 1977 *Manwatching* – the update is more than changing the non sexist title.)

You may find the study of facial expressions, and how they reflect emotions, more useful. A good starting point is:

Unmasking the Face
Paul Ekman and Wallace V. Friesen
(Malor Books, 2003, ISBN 1-883536-36-7)

Persuasion

Although I find some theories in this are superficial, unrealistic or just plain wrong, I have picked a selection, including some recent books that are of interest. They are included partly to show how this area is gathering interest with the public and therefore with the criminally minded. Many of the ideas are based on sound principles so are a useful read.

Changing Minds
Howard Gardner
(Harvard Business School, 2006, ISBN 1-4221-0329-3)

Influence – Science and Practice
Robert B. Cialdini
(Allyn and Bacon, 2001, ISBN 0-321-01147-3)

The Power of Persuasion
Robert Levine
(Oneworld, 2006, ISBN 978-1851684649)

Persuasion – The Art of Influencing People
James Borg
(Pearson Education, 2004, ISBN 0-273-68838-3)

Covert Persuasion
Kevin Hogan and James Speakman
(Wiley, 2006, ISBN 978-0470051412)

Unlimited Selling Power – How to Master Hypnotic Selling Skills
Donald Moine and Kenneth Lloyd
(Prentice Hall, 1990, ISBN 0-13-689126-8)

Persuasion Engineering
Richard Bandler and John LaValle
(Meta Publications, 1995, ISBN 978-0916990367)

The last one by Bandler is, as you would expect, a real gem.

Another recent release is:

YES! – 50 Secrets from the Science of Persuasion
Noah Goldstein, Steve Martin and Robert Cialdini
(Profile Books, 2007, ISBN 978-184668-016-8)

Secret number 33 is an interesting finding, with useful applications.

Derren Brown

I've given Derren a section of his own to reflect his genius. By applying many of the techniques I have explored in this book with 'magical artistry' and a focus on entertainment, Derren has created some classic moments. Significantly, he now has at his disposal the financial resources given by television to set up some wonderful set piece demonstrations. You should read everything he has written, even the earlier magic books are interesting to illustrate his background. And, you really should study his television work, from the simple, yet elegantly performed, handshake interrupt on Martin Bashir in one of his live shows, to the brain washing combination of NLP and hypnosis in *The Heist*, a master at work.

Tricks of the Mind
Derren Brown
(Channel 4 Books, 2006, ISBN 978-1-905-02626-5)

Not quite the great introduction to many of his techniques that it promises. Whilst not giving too much away, and a little ranting at times, it does allow you some insight into his use of hypnosis and NLP.

Other interesting books of his, from his early development also contain some insight:

Pure Effect – Direct Mindreading and Magical Artistry
Derren Brown
(H & R Magic Books, 2000) available direct from www.magicbookshop.com

Absolute Magic – A Model for Powerful Close-Up Performance
Derren Brown
(H & R Magic Books, 2003, ISBN 0-9727938-1-X)

Mind Expanding

An interesting title for these little offerings.

Think
Simon Blackburn
(Oxford University Press, 1999, ISBN 0-19-285425-9)

As a consultant, I spend many a night away from my family and often end up exploring bookshops for something interesting. One such time I ended up in the Philosophy section (it was probably next to Psychology!). Anyway, this little book offered thoughts on 'life, knowledge, consciousness, fate, God, truth, goodness and justice'. It does indeed make you think and saves you reading a small library of philosophy books.

Prometheus Rising
Robert Anton Wilson
(New Falcon, 1983, ISBN 1-56184-056-4)

Recommended to me by someone following one of my social engineering presentations, this book is a challenging, yet wonderfully entertaining, mixture of insight, intelligence and craziness. Each chapter has a series of sometime bizarre exercises, such as

- 'Accept this book, if not whole at least in general outlines. Assume you have been brainwashed' and

- 'Whenever you meet a young male or female, ask yourself consciously, "If it came to hand-to-hand combat, could I beat him/her?" Then try to determine how much of your behaviour is based on unconsciously asking and answering that question via pre-verbal body language.'

Blink – The Power of Thinking without Thinking
Malcolm Gladwell
(Penguin Books, 2006, ISBN 0-141-01459-8)

I loved this book, however I got frustrated with the author for not going beyond the observational and exploring the deeper process. However, if you get the depth from other books above, this has some great examples to analyse.

A work with a more academic focus, yet still very accessible, is:

Inevitable Illusions
Massimo Piattelli-Palmarini
(Wiley, 1994, ISBN 0-471-15962-X)

Below is another interesting little gem I found on my travels:

Mental Poisoning
H. Spencer Lewis
(The Rosicrucian Press, 1937)

Dedicated to the 'unfortunate men and women who have fallen prey to the poisoned darts of subtle, sordid, destructive suggestions'. An interesting work of its time that hints at thinking to come. However, its conclusions and advice should be taken with a healthy dose of:

The God Delusion
Richard Dawkins
(Bantam Press, 2006, ISBN 978-0-593-05548-9)

Essential reading for intelligent 'believers' and those who are just intelligent.

Information Security

I thought I had better include at least one information security book, so I thought this would be a good starting point for anyone wanting a non-technical (almost) approach to security with plenty of not-too-common sense. My original copy got taken to a hacking convention in Las Vagas by a colleague to get it signed by Bruce, and I never got it back! I presume he must have got it signed.

Secrets and Lies
Bruce Schneier
(Wiley, 2000, ISBN 0-471-25311-1)

Other

Obedience to Authority; An Experimental View
Stanley Milgram
(Harper & Row, 1974, ISBN 0-06-131983-X)

The Structure of Phenotypic Personality Traits
L.R. Goldberg
(American Psychologist, 1993, 48, 26–34)

Descartes' Error: Emotion, Reason, and the Human Brain
Antonio Damasio
(Putnam Publishing, 1994, ISBN 0-399-13894-3)

And Finally ...

Some people see him as a hacking hero, mistreated by the US judicial system, whilst others contend that it is wrong for convicted criminals to be making money on the back of their exploits. The cynics point to his focus on social engineering having more to do with his post-release restrictions on the use of computers, a little unfair given his, and other hackers, extensive use of social engineering techniques. However, I do recommend you consider buying:

The Art of Deception
Kevin D. Mitnick (and William L. Simon)
(Wiley, 2002, ISBN 0-471-23712-4)

Although superficial in psychological analysis, and short on countermeasures beyond the simple staff awareness approach, this book is packed full of simple examples that illustrate a range of social engineering vulnerabilities. Many of the stories are pure fiction, so expect a little exaggeration in places.

Index